How to Love a Black Woman

Also by Ronn Elmore

How to Love a Black Man

How to Love a Black Woman

GIVE—AND GET—THE VERY BEST IN YOUR RELATIONSHIP

Dr. Ronn Elmore

WARNER BOOKS

A Time Warner Company

Warner Books, Inc., 1271 Avenue of the Americas, New York, NY 10020
Visit our Web site at http://warnerbooks.com

 A Time Warner Company

Printed in the United States of America
First Printing: August 1998
10 9 8 7 6 5 4 3 2 1

Library of Congress Cataloging-in-Publication Data

Elmore, Ronn.
    How to love a Black woman : give and get the very best in your
relationship / Ronn Elmore.
        p. cm.
    ISBN 0-446-52281-3
    1. Man-woman relationships—United States. 2. Afro-American
women—Psychology. 3. Afro-American men—Psychology. 4. Intimacy
(Psychology) I. Title.
HQ801.E43   1998   97-31311
158.2—dc21
                                                              CIP

Book design: H Roberts Design

To the Lord Jesus Christ,
who daily tutors me in the lessons of love.
And to Aladrian, the best homework
a man could ever hope for.

Table of Contents

How to Love a Black Woman

Introduction

No, this is *not* "one of *those* books." Contrary to what images a quick glance at the title may stir, THE BOOK YOU ARE NOW HOLDING IS DEFINITELY *NOT* ABOUT:

- How to pick up Black women, anywhere, anytime, *or*
- How to satisfy Black women in bed, and keep them coming back for more, *or*
- How to keep the Black woman in your life from ever getting mad at you, *or*
- How to "score points" and get anything you want from a Black woman.

Loving Black women with wisdom, sensitivity, and skillfulness is what this book is all about. It's focused on the near limitless power you have to give and get the very best—spiritually, physically, mentally, and emotionally—in your relationship with her.

Make no mistake. Loving another person, any other person, is a job. It's a profoundly appealing job and one that many of us take quite seriously. But it is a job. And as is the case with any job you are working to excel at, discovering ways to do it even more capably, and to get even greater results, is the goal. The quality of your love, and your effectiveness at expressing it to the Black woman in your life (or the one on her way), is one of the key measures of our manhood.

The fact that you are reading this book suggests to me that you have much in common with countless men I have met through my counseling practice, seminars, and on radio and television talk shows, in addition to the men who have written me since the release of my earlier book, *How to Love a Black Man*.

I find them to be, like me, men who already love Black women and who have every intention of continuing to. They are both married and single men, brash but sincere young upstarts, and brothers who have been on the job for much longer than a hot minute. What they have in common is that they have become tired of all the drama that surrounds Black male-female relationships—the finger-pointing back and forth, the mistrust and hostility that divides us along gender lines, and, of course, the statistics that are constantly trotted out to dramatize the hopeless state of affairs that supposedly exists between Black men and women.

In spite of it all, they are men who are captivated by the best of Black women's strength and dignity, and the infinite ways in which their beauty is manifest. They continue to feel honored by the admiration, respect, and support that their women have lavished upon them. And they are men who are still wholly committed to contributing powerfully and meaningfully to her life as well.

Men do that best when they are sure they know the answer to this fundamental question: "What exactly does she want and need from me?" The pages ahead provide the answers to that question. And when you are armed with clear answers, deeper satisfaction in love is available to both of you.

When I say "love," I'm talking about a balanced and deliberate commitment to another person, one that is demonstrated by action. Action that benefits your mate without discounting yourself. Action that is caring, creative, and consistent, without being self-devaluing, manipulative, or self-centered.

And when I say "satisfaction," I mean the abiding contentment and confidence that result from committing to love someone, being loved in return, and knowing and doing the actions that most effectively demonstrate that love. That's *the job,* and for men, deep satisfaction comes from doing it extremely well.

This book will tell you what women say they need and want from us—but it will also explain it, and, most importantly, apply it in the "language of men," which is:

- Logical and concrete rather than abstract and inconclusive.
- Constructive and compelling rather than critical and condemning.
- Practical and goal-oriented rather than theoretical and unattainable.
- Simple and concise rather than complicated and repetitive.

Women have not always known exactly how to get their points across to their men, with the kind of directness and clarity that helps unlock our highest intentions and our most determined efforts. We *hear* them, but we can't swear we always *understand* what they want, why they want it, and what they want us to do about it. And if you don't understand that, even when you're willing to give it, you're very likely to miss the mark anyway.

Men *need* answers. We need them so we can draw conclusions, so we can feel confident that we understand, and, ultimately, so that we can perform effectively. Since you were a little boy, you wanted answers. When something was broken, you wanted to know how to fix it. If something was working just fine, you wanted to know why it was, and what you could do to make it work even better. Men don't ever want to be left in the dark, without answers about anything that we've got to deal with. That's especially true when it comes to our love lives.

Men are inherently possessors of the characteristics and inclinations of a conqueror-adventurer. You are not the sort to rise to a challenge or set sail on a course without first observing, analyzing, and assessing what you are trying to do and what obstacles stand in the way of getting it done—excellently. Having solid facts—in advance—is what men want, and probably always will.

Straight facts are the basis of your confidence. When you are confident, you get all kinds of good things done. Men treasure the sense of empowerment that comes from confidence. Having the facts helps us to get it.

Think about it. When you are engaged in any endeavor in which your confidence level is high, your commitment level tends to be high as well. Conversely, when you aren't confident that you know enough, or have enough of what you need to excel, your commitment can easily wane. That's because for you, commitment is a direct by-product of confidence.

If you're a man who ever did, does now, or ever will love a Black woman, you have probably already heard more than you wanted to hear about what they expect of the men in their lives, how hard a time they've had getting it, and how angry they are about it. Black women, no longer willing to settle for vague hopes of love's "payday, someday," are challenging the men in their lives to offer a more sensitive, demonstrative, consistent love that delivers as promised. After hearing women's requests, demands, complaints, and criticisms, some men have begun to believe that Black women are *never* satisfied, and never will be. But if you believe that, before long you could get the idea that it's not even worth it to try. And if it's not worth it to try—or to try again and again—then attempting to apply the advice you'll find here will be an exercise in futility. All pain and no gain.

But we men must also take responsibility for the ways we have indeed flunked. All of us, at one time or another, have been guilty of giving less than love's best to some Black woman, or several. For a multitude of reasons, some simple, others very complex, we have displayed everything from self-seeking, self-protecting, and self-justifying to short attention spans, poor discipline, broken promises, and the tendency to drift. Of course you know men who are more guilty of these offenses than are you. But all of us have, at some time or another, compromised ourselves and blown it. And too often, rather than acknowledge it, and repent of our offense against her, we have responded with defensiveness, blame, or utter silence. All of these have wounded our women and misrepresented our highest intentions.

But *How to Love a Black Woman* is not merely a critique of what's wrong with us in love. It is a celebration of what's right with us, and how to make it better than ever.

Nothing you'll read here is meant to imply that Black men and women are plagued with certain unconquerable psychological, behavioral, or relational dysfunctions that are only found in our race and culture. I have not written with that erroneous belief in mind, and I caution you not to read it with that in mind either. The fact is, getting and keeping a meaningful and mutually satisfying love relationship is no easier or harder for Black folk than anybody else.

But even our best skills can stand to be sharpened. Though they may seem to have stood the test of time, our most brilliant insights about the opposite sex can always be polished to a yet higher gleam. This book will further sharpen your skills in reading the heart of your woman—not just hearing her words, or observing her behavior and reacting to it. I suspect that often, when we don't have the fullest understanding of what's in their hearts, we miss our women's deepest needs of us, and respond only to what we *think* they mean, which may be far different from what they actually meant. Everything you'll find ahead is designed to help you *know*, not think, assume, hope, or guess, but *know*.

For too long, too many of us have secretly held the belief that women are the more qualified experts on loving. If we are honest, we'll admit that we often tend to take our cues from them, assuming that, when it comes to matters of the heart, women are always the ones who know the "right" way.

That belief is responsible for our style of loving becoming reduced to finding out what they think we ought to be doing and doing it just that way (or at least something that we think will look like it to them). Even when it "works" (meaning our women liked it, and they let us know they did), we have eventually come away strangely dissatisfied. We are haunted by the uneasy suspicion that, if we're just dancing to her music, then she's got our noses wide open!

Maybe it was woven into our masculine souls at creation. Or perhaps it's the legacy handed down to us from our tribesmen forefathers. But the fact is, men rise to their highest levels of excellence in any endeavor—especially love—based on definitions, standards, and models of functioning that have been established by other men. Men empower men. Literally or symbolically, we have each stood as one man amongst a million men, and have been challenged to recommit to a standard of integrity and excellence that includes how we love our women.

How to Love a Black Woman is written by a man, for men. It is, of course, appreciative of what our women are asking of us and needing from us. But it is no less appreciative of what you need and how you feel, think, and function, and what it takes for you to remain true to yourself.

Simply put, if you act on the no-nonsense, practical advice found here, not only will your understanding of Black women and your love for them grow, but you will grow personally, as well.

I promise no magic formula or "one-size-fits-all" solutions here, but you should expect these practical principles to work, and to work well.

I'm sure they will, if you will.

PART I

The Straight Facts

Your Phenomenal Woman: Who She Really Is and Isn't

The Straight Facts

Whatever your own personal images and perceptions about the nature of Black women are, they will stare you straight in the face as you read this book. You will find that some of those images of her will be confirmed here and you will take pleasure in knowing that, in that specific area, you have been working with solid, reliable facts that have helped you to relate effectively to the Black woman in your life.

However, there are likely to be other images and perceptions about them that you may hold which, as you read this book, will be challenged for their accuracy and their usefulness in your efforts to love her in a way that benefits you both. These faulty, albeit perhaps well-meaning, misperceptions can be seen for what they are, and some more accurate and thus more useful ones will replace them.

Remember: How you perceive Black women has everything to do with how you will relate to them (and of course, how they will relate back to you).

For the next few pages, you will have the opportunity to fine-tune your own image of Black women.

If you are honest and open-minded, and willing to boldly examine your own thinking, this section will benefit you greatly. Here you'll take inventory of the facts you have and how well they have served you in the adventure of loving a Black woman.

As I share with you some of men's most commonly held images of Black women, ask yourself constantly:

Is this image truthful?
Is this image fair?
Is this image respectful?
Is this image useful?
Is this image mine?

The Fits on Me Black Woman

From somewhere beyond a sincere brother's hopes, high standards, and way beyond reality, comes the phenomenal female of myth and legend, the Fits on Me Black Woman. In spite of the fact that she really doesn't exist, she's perceived as perfection personified and many a man either thought he had seen one locked on to some other brother's arm, or that he had one himself, only to eventually discover that he had been (once again) sadly mistaken. The Fits on Me Black Woman possesses every impressive quality you'd ever want, and not a thing you don't. She fits our fantasies like a glove, and holds the promise of being worth the very long wait for her glorious arrival. Their superior good taste and limitless patience is what keeps some men eternally searching for her, while repeatedly dismissing the real-life women all around them. If a man believes in the existence of the Fits on Me Black Woman, then his woman has to fit all his idealized "got to's."

- She's *"gotta"* be incredibly, completely, eternally fine, with no visible flaws, thus perfectly fitting his lofty daydreams about himself.
- She's *"gotta"* be an absolute genius, with the kind of brilliance and extraordinary ability that elevates his status. She fits him, because her brilliance can be turned on and off—and he controls the switch.
- She's *"gotta"* be extroverted enough to prove he's snagged a winner, but introverted enough to keep others from thinking he picked a tramp. She fits him because she's willing to become what he dreams up.
- She's *"gotta"* be interested in what he's interested in, to the same degree that he is. She fits him because she doesn't place a high value on things he doesn't care about.
- She's *"gotta"* be highly spiritual, but she fits him by not letting pleasing her God become more important than pleasing her man.
- She's *"gotta"* be honest and outspoken, but she fits him by only saying what he loves to hear.
- She's *"gotta"* be ambitious and self-reliant, but she fits him because she's willing to trash her ambitions and goals if they inconvenience or intimidate him.
- She's *"gotta"* be passionate and sexually proficient, but she fits him because she's willing to let him decide the when and how of it all.
- She's *"gotta"* intuitively know his values, desires, and expectations, but she fits him because she doesn't need him to tell her what they are.
- She's *"gotta"* have all the nurturing qualities of his mother, but she fits him because she never treats him like he's her son.

Obviously this image of Black women is the figment of a highly creative, but completely self-absorbed, imagination. It's a naive and unrealistic stereotype of Black women that characterizes them as their men's perfect trophies, and the ultimate badge of his status and significance. But the Fits on Me image of Black women is way over the top. The facts are way off, and to use them will keep you endlessly waiting for the "right" Black woman to come along and constantly dissatisfied with the real-life one you already have.

THIS IS NOT WHO BLACK WOMEN REALLY ARE

The Steps on Me Black Woman

Far out at the opposite extreme from the previous fantasized portrait of Black women is the Steps on Me Black Woman. She is that hopelessly negative woman that embodies men's worst perceptions. It's an overgeneralized misrepresentation of all Black women, based on the most glaring faults of some of them. This distorted image of them has helped make Black male-female relations increasingly become a hotbed of mistrust, hostility, and alienation.

- She competes with men, trying hard to outdo them in nearly every area, including love, career, finances, morality, and self-sufficiency. And she feels justified in pointing out how men come up short in them all.
- She's never satisfied, and constantly demands more and more sensitivity and emotional expression from her man, then criticizes him for being "weak" and coming up short when he gives it.
- She's critical, comparing her man unfavorably to men of other races and cultures, and delights in showing him how he comes up short.
- She's suspicious, convinced that her man means her no

good and either just lied to, cheated on, or disrespected her, or is about to somehow come up short integrity-wise.

- She's unfaithful and either has had, or is secretly fantasizing about having, some other man, against whom her man comes up short.
- She's bitchy, all neck-swiveling, hip-holding, eye-rolling, and acid-tongued when he fails. She believes when he comes up short, he deserves it.

Are there any Black women who possess these harsh, judgmental qualities? Absolutely. But does this image accurately reflect the way most Black women relate to their men? Of course not. Your disgust with them and perhaps some exhausted unwillingness to take a closer look at Black women and the nature, intent, and meaning of their style of relating may threaten to lock this scathing generalization into your mind. In fact, few women deserve to be placed in this category. It is as extreme and unrealistic as the previous one.

THIS IS NOT WHO BLACK WOMEN REALLY ARE

The Leans on Me Black Woman

The Leans on Me Black Woman is yet another worthless misrepresentation of the facts. It's sure to steer you down a dead-end street rather than reliably guide you through the adventure of mutually gratifying love with a Black woman. This distortion of Black women's image is based on the suspicion that some men hold, which suggests that:

- She *needs* me to make her life work.
- She *needs* me to take away all her hurts.

- She *needs* me to fulfill her romantic fantasies.
- She *needs* me to finance her existence.
- She *needs* me to give her a reason to live.
- She *needs* a minimum of 200 percent of me for her to feel loved and secure.

"Emotionally dependent," "smothering," and "insecure" are words that describe this image of Black women that many men hold. Reading all Black women this way can cause you to view them as an energy-depleting burden who need way too much from you. She overwhelms you with responsibility for her needs. Or, equally bad, she's exactly what you desire, because when she leans on you, you feel like Superman! But what you may interpret as "terminal neediness" in her could be the manifestation of a woman's natural pursuit of a vital sense of stability and security in her relationship with you. To a man, her determined pursuit of a mutual and interdependent connection with you can easily be mislabeled as "emotional disability."

THIS IS NOT WHO BLACK WOMEN REALLY ARE

The Works on Me Black Woman

Maybe you're a man whose internal video image and personal dictionary definition of Black women is closer to the Works on Me Black Woman, with all her ridiculously high standards, precise tastes, and unceasing preoccupation with making improvements upon the man in her life:

- She's determined to make her man suit her ideals, her fantasies, and her agenda.
- She's full to overflowing, with unsolicited advice and

subtle or overt attempts to instruct the man who loves her.

- She's chronically controlling, a walking book of rules and regulations that she expects her man to follow explicitly, if his love is sincere.
- She can't seem to "connect" romantically when her man's pace or performance does not match her preferences.
- She thinks his job is to find out what she wants him to do or be, and immediately get in step with it.
- She talks too much and listens too little.
- She's pushy, manipulative, bossy, and vengeful.
- She expects her man's love to be demonstrated by bowing to her standards, values, and expectations.
- She's a combination schoolteacher, mother, and foreman.

The Works on Me Black Woman image could be firmly embedded in your psyche due to even a single previous experience with a "compulsive controller." But beware, it can also come from inside you, if you tend to have a hard time accepting Black women who really aren't compulsive improvers, but are assertive, self-assured women who do not fail to voice their desires, expectations, and opinions. And if they sound to you like demands or instructions, it can feel as if your competence to achieve results on your own is inadequate.

THIS IS NOT WHO BLACK WOMEN REALLY ARE

Left with only the four previous perceptions of Black women, you may find the idea of developing and maintaining intimate relationships with them a not so appetizing proposition. With those stereotyped generalizations, loving a Black woman will be a start-again, stop-again, can't-wait-to-get-in, then can't-wait-to-get-out nightmare. The four images of Black women outlined above are actually distortions. Though it's not hard to see how these images have come to persuade us of their accuracy, they are untrue. They steer us away from mutually satisfying love, rather than toward it.

Take a closer look. Something is definitely wrong with these pictures.

I want to offer you a more balanced, comprehensive, and realistic view of real-life Black women than any of the previous ones. It comes closest to the straight facts, and not those rare, one-time-only experiences that aren't even close to the norm. And straight facts are what men rely upon in love, as in everything else.

The Counts on Me Black Woman

- She treasures spiritual, physical, emotional, and psychological intimacy with her man, which may sometimes appear to him as "clingy neediness." Mutuality and demonstrative affection are key. She treasures balance and therefore keeps close tabs on the score.
- She is at her best in relationships when she is confident of her man's devotion, faithfulness, and consistency—as demonstrated, not merely declared.
- She often speaks first from her subjective world of feelings, then from her precise, objective awareness.
- She has a love style that relies heavily on verbal expression.
- She has high expectations of her man and of loving relationships, which may appear too much like "demands to perform" to him.
- She can give almost limitless love, encouragement, and affection to her man when she is secure in her man's love for her.

- She can feel the need to withdraw, defend, or retaliate if she experiences fatigue, frustration, and the fear of being rejected, ignored, or taken advantage of.
- She has become increasingly more cautious and less trusting about showing vulnerability to the men in her life.

Contrary to appearances, and some of men's most fiercely held beliefs, the Counts on Me Black Woman is who really exists in the heart and soul of the woman in your life. More than likely, that's who the Black woman you have loved in the past, the one you love now, or will love in the future really is. Admittedly, it is not always easy to detect her presence inside your mate. The Counts on Me Black Woman comes in all shapes and sizes and hues, with every possible personality type and behavioral trait. To truly see her, you will sometimes need to look beyond a woman's tone and attitude, or hear the words she *didn't* speak, or respond to the feelings she failed to express. It can completely transform your picture of her.

She wants, above all, to be able to depend on you for the steady, willing supply of your very best treasures—your sincere and demonstrated devotion and commitment.

She doesn't *need* you, in the "can't make it without you" sense, any more than you need her. She deeply *desires* you, and the love you are able to bring into her life.

To attempt to give her that love while holding on to the distorted images and stereotypes means you'd be working in the dark, without the real facts. You'd labor in vain trying to give and get real love without the good understanding that matters so much to men.

You have, there inside you, abundant power that, when properly harnessed and creatively applied, can make incredibly fulfilling love possible for both of you.

Believing that will make all the difference in the world, as you navigate your way through this book. Because now the straight facts are in:

THIS IS WHO BLACK WOMEN REALLY ARE

Like AM and FM

Men have repeatedly told me that when it comes to loving Black women they feel as if we speak two different languages, come from different planets, or are on different wavelengths. They are right. And it's perfectly okay that we are. You see, with men and women, aside from the fact that both are of the human species, nearly everything else about them is as different as night is from day.

In terms of quality of character, neither gender is inherently better or worse than the other. When I say *different*, I'm not talking about what's good or bad, normal or abnormal. I'm talking about somebody else's perfectly valid way of being that doesn't always match your own.

But even if you say you accept that fact, yet you fail to understand *how* these differences play out in your relationship, it'll be next to impossible to create a relationship that's fulfilling to you both.

In the course of loving a Black woman, a lightbulb may have come on and you've gotten the revelation that the things that mean the most to her in the realm of romance are often far different from the things that mean the most to you. Therefore, how she expects you to demonstrate your love and commitment to her is vastly different from what you expect from her. You've seen this principle in operation when something that truly thrills or saddens her honestly has nothing like that effect on you. Or that what she does when stressed out or in conflict with you usually doesn't match your style at all.

Much of this is not because of the *kind* of woman she is, or the kind of man you are. It's because she's a woman and you are a man—and the two of you are "wired" quite differently.

Whether you've noticed it previously or are considering it for the first time now, you have made an all-important discovery: that Black women and the men who love them are just like AM and FM radio. Though we have our similarities, you'll never hear exactly the same programming on one that you do on the other.

By saying we're on different frequencies, I mean that you and your woman have two distinctly different internal driving forces as primary motivators (i.e., the thing that matters most to you, and how you are naturally inclined to go after it). Your driving force is the thing that propels you and what explains, in a broad sense, why you relate in life and in love the way you do.

For women in love relationships, the internal driving force is the high-priority pursuit of an overall sense of *security* (i.e., stability, harmony, and intimacy). She is at her best in life, and particularly in relationships, when she feels secure that "everything is going to be okay"; and that your desire for her, commitment to her, and intimate bond with her cannot be easily broken. To her, satisfaction is spelled: s-e-c-u-r-i-t-y. Think of women as being on the FM frequency.

Men, on the other hand, have a different, but no less significant, internal driving force. Our primary motivation is the high-priority pursuit of an overall sense of *significance* (i.e., competency, admiration, approval, and self-confidence).

To you, real satisfaction comes from significance. Think of men as being on the AM frequency.

The Black woman you love is happiest, most content, and most fulfilled when you've (perhaps without even knowing it) scratched her itch for security. She's been at her worst when you've ignored, insensitively treated, and looked down on her for having that need. She flourishes when you consistently prove that you treasure her and are thoroughly devoted to her emotional, physical, psychological, and spiritual well-being. When she senses that you care about what's in her best interest as much as your own, and, above all, when she's confident that you are not going to kick her to the curb, she relaxes. She is secure. She exhales.

You, on the other hand, find that kind of deep satisfaction when you feel assured that you have her respect, admiration, and appreciation.

We hate to fail. We're instinctively prone to avoid it, at almost any cost, because we shun anything that we perceive as a threat to our sense of significance. On the AM frequency, blame, disapproval, ridicule, and self-doubt are our relentless adversaries.

One effective way to get a clearer picture of a Black woman's internal driving force is to contrast the key components of her frequency with those of your own.

Now here's where it gets tricky. How can she get from you the kind of love that fits her FM frequency when you're on an altogether different one? And, if you do manage to give what she needs, how can you be sure you'll get from her what fits your AM frequency?

The fact to remember is, you are much more likely to get the kind of approving, affirming, admiring love your frequency is tuned to if you give the kind of sensitive, supportive, stable kind of love your woman needs. Real-life love has a mathematical law of reciprocity that's constantly at work. Give

Men Are on AM **The Key Features of** **His *Significance* Agenda**	**Women Are on FM** **The Key Features of** **Her *Security* Agenda**
Consistent applause for what he does	Constant affection for who she is
The ability to control his emotions	The freedom to express her emotions
Nonverbal demonstration	Verbal communication
Being effective at improving how things look	Being effective at improving how things feel
Mastery of applied logic	Master of applied intuition
Well-developed high-quality achievements	Well-developed high-quality relationships
Attentive to the possibilities of the future	Attentive to the realities of the past
Feeling that he's needed	Feeling that she's wanted
Focused on where we're trying to go (the goal/destination)	Focused on how we're trying to go (the process/means)

her more of her kind, get back more of your kind. It doesn't even matter which of you starts first, the results tend to be the same.

Even a superficial examination of the respective features of the two frequencies helps you understand how it is that Black women and their men have been reaching out for each other, yet too often sadly missing each other, failing to sustain an intimate connection. In fact, my years of clinical work with couples indicate that a large percentage of the confusion, anger, and disillusionment that sometimes keeps Black women from trusting your love, and sometimes keeps you from wanting to offer it, is because both men and women have not known about, allowed for, or adequately responded to each other's very different frequencies.

Sensitively and skillfully responding to her security agenda doesn't mean disposing of your significance agenda. (It's impossible for a man to do that anyway!) It does mean loving her will challenge you to give, do, and be with her in ways that strengthen and enhance her sense of security in you, in the relationship, and in herself.

In my previous book, *How to Love a Black Man,* I took Black women on a guided tour of the characteristics of your frequency, and how they should expect it to show up in relationships with you. I also explained to them the practical and mutually beneficial ways they should relate to you that could help you both get the satisfaction you desire and deserve.

Now it's your turn.

The bottom line is, you can't serve her from the same menu of delicacies that feeds your masculine hunger for significance and expect it to nourish and satisfy her hunger for security. It's a major mistake to assume that what you love to get from love is what you should dole out to her. Even if you give her the very best of what you freely give to other men, and they give to you, you will not have met the "dietary requirements" of a security-seeking woman by doing so.

FM Puts Up a Fight and AM Takes Flight

You can huff, puff, and sweat with the utmost sincerity to offer the Black woman in your life your preferred kind of love, but if you're only giving out the kind you like to take in, it's nearly the same to her as saying, "You don't matter to me!"

The hurt and rejection that result from that sincere but misdirected approach to love can easily and automatically switch on her "fight impulse"—the urge to blame, bash, and berate you as a self-defense against attacks on her sense of security, as well as a way to launch an offensive assault on you.

Since the closeness and connection of intimacy feeds her security hunger, if she can't achieve that feeling with you in

What Men Offer to Other Men They Care About	How Women Might Perceive It When It's Offered to Them	What Women Want from Men Instead
PRIVACY AND INDEPENDENCE *"Let me leave you alone to figure out that problem of yours. I'll know you need me when you call for me."*	**ABANDONED IN A CRISIS** *"You pulled away, leaving me alone when I most needed you."*	**ON-SITE SUPPORT** *"I want you to want to be intimately attached to me in this problem/ experience."*
COLLABORATION THROUGH COMPETITION *"We're both doing it. We'll both do it better if we try to do it better than each other."*	**SELFISH RIVALRY** *"It can't be us together when it's you against me. You'd rather win alone than with me."*	**COLLABORATION THROUGH INTERDEPENDENCE** *"I want to be a part of an 'Us,' not just a 'Me.'"*
HIGH RESPECT FOR VISIBLE ABILITIES AND ACCOMPLISHMENTS *"Bravo! Man, you worked it, won it, and whipped it. You are so good at that."*	**MISPLACED PRIORITIES** *"Wait a minute. Don't feelings, dreams, and intentions matter to you? Am I only important based on what I do or have?"*	**PASSION FOR HER AS A PERSON REGARDLESS OF HER PERFORMANCE** *"I long for you to love me, not just approve of me."*
GOAL-ORIENTED ADVICE AND CRITICISM *"Brother, you shouldn't do it like that. Your way won't work. Let me tell you what you should do instead. . . ."*	**BLAME AND REJECTION** *"Why must you be so critical? Can't you see I'm trying?"*	**MORE FOCUS ON HER GOOD INTENTIONS RATHER THAN ON SOLUTIONS AND OUTCOMES** *"I don't want to lose your love if I don't follow your advice."*
THE BLUNT LITERAL TRUTH *(Function over Feelings)* *"Actually I think it looks ridiculous."*	**CARELESS INSENSITIVITY** *"It's not so much what you say; I have a hard time with the way you say it."*	**GENTLY CONVEYED TRUTH** *(Feelings over Function)* *"You speak so sensitively to me, I must matter to you."*
MEANINGFUL SILENCE *(When They Are Content)* *"All is well between us, so what is there to talk about?"*	**SHUT-OUT** *"When people care about each other, they talk about themselves. You're not talking, so you must not care."*	**FREQUENT UNSOLICITED VERBAL DISCLOSURE** *"I feel like I'm so special to you when you volunteer to share more of your thoughts and feelings."*
THE RIGHT TO "RUN HOT AND COLD" *"Hey man, where have you been keeping yourself all these months? I know I haven't called or come by either, but it's sure good to see you again."*	**INSTABILITY, INATTENTIVENESS, AND LACK OF COMMITMENT** *"You're not as intense about me or our relationship as you once were. If you really cared for me, it would be impossible to become distracted."*	**STEADY, CONSISTENT EMOTIONAL INTENSITY** *"Your love really is here to stay. I feel secure."*

love, she's apt to try it in war. At least in war, her pained insides tell her, we are fully engaged together and focused on each other. It's a negative form of intimacy.

So when she is in fight mode, she'll tend to relate to you in a way that sends the message that "you are a no-good man." Now your sense of significance is assaulted. You feel the dreaded loss of esteem, and your sense of goodness and competence are in jeopardy. Feelings of failure seep in. Your automatic response? Flight. Finding a way out, by withdrawing, unplugging, and disconnecting, is what feels right, safe, and necessary. Physically, mentally, or emotionally you are likely to "check out" when your flight impulse is triggered.

When you take flight, her sense of security is profoundly injured—which can trigger her fight impulse. In turn, she'll be inclined to cease from offering you any more of the approval, applause, or admiration you thrive on, and you'll fly away even further, bringing less and less of yourself to the relationship. As her hurt feelings, and your mutual disdain for each other, intensify, she may also employ, in "fight mode," scolding, punishments, and dismissal. All of which sends the message that there is something wrong with you. Thus she effectively frustrates your sense of significance and triggers your "flight" response. And back and forth it goes.

In a self-perpetuating, circular, yet sometimes completely undetectable pattern, the fighting and the fleeing—both subtle and overt—can go on and on forever. Like AM and FM, on two different frequencies we can go right on missing each other's love in whole or in part.

It is essential that you take a closer look at what's uniquely important to the Black woman you love or one day will, and the dynamic interplay between her primary motivation and yours. I suspect your mind has already begun to do what men's minds do once they spot a problem: (a) We try to break the problem down into smaller, more manageable pieces, and (b) We systematically develop strategies targeted to those various pieces, one by one, until we conquer the whole. It's your natural and very powerful way to analyze problems, rise to challenges, and effect change in your life.

This Is How We Do It

Before we rush headlong into the security-building how to's for loving a Black woman, you'd do well to take an honest look at yourself and your approach to love. How effective is your characteristic style of relating to Black women? How well has it worked to foster a genuine sense of security in her and genuine significance in you? Have you seen the same dead-end patterns played out repeatedly in your relationship, where only the names have been changed—the stories are only reruns of your last relationship and the one before that and the one before that. . . . Or are you married or in an established long-term relationship where nobody's packing up to go anywhere, but neither of you are giving or getting much fulfillment or have any sense that your love is climbing to ever higher levels?

When we take a closer look at our own approaches to love, we often discover how easy it is to unknowingly sabotage the very satisfaction we desire in our relationships. You can get in your own way and set yourself up for disappointment. It's easy to do, hard to recognize, and harder still to admit.

The big drawback with love is that to do it right means you consume lots of time, and expend lots of energy, all the while running the risk that you could become distracted, misunderstood, or exposed as a novice. Love makes even strong, confident men vulnerable to the possibility of criticism, fatigue, and failure, and the erosion of self-esteem that goes with it. On top of that, love offers no up-front guarantees that you will be loved in return. It's very risky business. Contrary to popular misconceptions, men do want fulfilling love and solid relationships no less than do women. But the risks can make pursuing deeper levels of love with a Black woman seem complicated, uncertain, burdensome, and thus continually unsatisfying.

Love Substitutes

In an attempt to minimize the risks, avoid the pain of failure, and conserve mental and emotional energy, many men have opted for a safer alternative to real-life love—love substitutes. Love substitutes are the well-ingrained thought and behavior patterns that you may have adopted over the years. Though they can talk, look, act, and feel like genuine love, they really aren't at all. They come from a distorted view of masculinity, of women or their expectations of you, your expectations of yourself, and often from the hidden obsession with protecting and preserving your sense of significance at all costs.

Using love substitutes instead of the real thing works well to decrease the risk level in your relationships with Black women. But love substitutes never work to build long-term mutual satisfaction. They are, however, powerfully appealing. Just ahead I will introduce you to the five most common love substitutes. Your version of one or more of them could be exactly what you have used unknowingly and repeatedly in your relationships with women.

How exactly do love substitutes work? Consider this.

Your perception of what it means to be a man is based largely on positive performance. How you see yourself and discern your significance is often linked to knowing the right thing to do, the right way to do it, and getting the right response for having done it. Deep on the inside, men have imprinted in us the idea that being a good man means doing a good job and getting a good response from those who see them do it. There is no place where a man wants more to be right, good, and thus significant, than in the eyes of his woman. How you define what it means to be a good man and how you think you live up to that standard will always affect how you choose to present yourself and relate to women.

I have found that many men have distorted perceptions—either a little or a lot—of themselves and the basis for their significance, as well as distorted perceptions of women and their expectations. These distortions arise from our experiences, upbringing, erroneous or incomplete self-definitions, as well as from our own emotional baggage. If your perception of manhood and of women's expectations is off target, what you expect and how you relate to women will be also. Which makes you susceptible to picking up one or more ineffective and ultimately self-sabotaging love substitutes.

If you think the way to win a woman's applause and avoid her displeasure with you is to only let her see your shiny parts, never your rusty ones, instead of loving them you can easily become obsessed with charming them—your love substitute.

If you're a *Charmer,* having a woman who stays utterly impressed with most everything about you is how you work to get applause and its vital by-product, significance. You shape, for her, a perfectly positive image that is sure to send her head over heels for you. But when she gets close enough to see your imperfections and her standing ovations get fewer, you tend to "get out of Dodge" and start your one-man show all over again elsewhere. Instead of satisfaction, you feel *fear of being exposed*.

If you see Black women as the raw material that you can mold into the kind of trophy companion who'll get you plenty of the sense of esteem and self-importance you yearn for, instead of loving them, you may be prone to improving them—your love substitute.

If you're an *Improver,* you will only have use for the woman who is willing to let you transform her into an impressive extension of your own identity. When others see her as special, she is acceptable according to your blueprint, and you get the applause you crave. But when she stops submitting to your suggestions, though, you have little use for her and start searching for another "fixer-upper" project. Instead of satisfaction, you feel *unappreciated*.

If you see Black women as insecure, overemotional, self-absorbed, undependable, overaggressive, or any other characteristics that men are highly allergic to, instead of loving them you may tend to blame them—your love substitute.

If you're a *Blamer,* you believe that whatever minor faults you may have are far outweighed by what you see as the major dysfunction in her. You uphold your sense of significance by casting yourself as mostly right and women as mostly wrong. Like a saintly and long-suffering martyr you endure her glaring deficiencies, or you give her a life sentence locked away from your love. Instead of satisfaction, you feel *seething resentment*.

If you see women as the "real" authorities on love and what your role should be in the relationship, and if you see yourself as responsible for living up to their demands, you will be tempted to overgive—your love substitute.

If you're a *Giver,* you're constantly working to be and do

whatever you think she requires. Your significance agenda tells you that her disappointment or dissatisfaction will shrink you to nothingness. Instead of satisfaction, you feel *responsible for everything*.

If you see Black women as unruly, immature, and inferior to you, and if you see yourself as The Man, whose job it is to direct the process and control the outcomes of everything, you are likely to lean toward ruling—your love substitute.

If you're a *Ruler,* you maintain your significance by establishing a dictatorship and requiring her unquestioning submission to it. To you, manhood means not just having power, but having power over somebody else. Instead of satisfaction, you feel *pressure to perform*.

Men who have adopted love substitutes may be very sincere in the "love" they offer. They call it love, but love that comes from Charmers, Improvers, Blamers, Givers, and Rulers is only a counterfeit version of the real thing. Love substitutes end up keeping Black women and the men who love them apart—even in the same home. They never make for lasting satisfaction for either of you. They may help you feel pride, efficiency, control, or esteem, but never abiding satisfaction. They can't. Love substitutes arise out of concern for yourself, not the other person. Your mate then responds by "loving" you in some equally self-serving way. Selfishness is the opposite of love.

This may explain why it sometimes seemed so impossible to make loving a Black woman work and last. She's looked out for her security needs, and you've looked out for your significance needs; and both of you have tried to play it safe by using an imitation form of love.

Without knowing our own self-sabotaging patterns we are completely focused on our mate's relational flaws. Loving a Black woman begins to look like too much of a bother. Other endeavors, like making money and getting famous, appear to be better uses of your time and energy. Then the devastation caused by love substitutes is complete. Another Black man's and another Black woman's souls become strangers to each other.

It is important to note that the love substitutes listed here and in the following pages are generalizations—and, in some cases, exaggerated ones at that. They won't describe your personal style word for word or quirk for quirk, but much of what you find under one or more of these five headings will probably describe you fairly closely in some area. Don't check out. Keep your focus and this could be your chance to do a total overhaul or just to work on some needed finishing touches in your approach to loving your woman. Recognizing the patterns that don't work in your relationship is the first step toward establishing patterns that do.

In the next section we will take a closer look at these five most common love substitutes (there are probably a million more!). If you are bold and honest, you will be able to identify the one or ones that apply to you. Of course, none of the love substitute categories say all there is to say about one person's relationship patterns, and virtually no man uses only one of these substitutes. Typically we are all "combination counterfeiters." But watch closely for whatever may hold even a few threads of truth about you and your style of loving up to this point in your life. These may be the very threads that, with a little tug, will make your previously unidentified love substitute(s) come completely unraveled.

Although it may be tempting to skip these pages and go directly to the action-oriented Policies and Procedures, resist. First face your own love substitutes head-on, through the descriptive profiles, the brief analysis, and the self-tests in the next chapter. That, combined with a reexamination of your perceptions of Black women, will make the Policies and Procedures much more meaningful and of more strategic benefit.

In Part II, all seventy Policies and Procedures will have one or more symbols above the title, representing each love substitute. By the time you get there, you will know well which love substitute(s) is (are) yours. Watch closely. Wherever your symbol(s) appears, it is indicating a Policy or Procedure that you should consider a high priority.

The Five Most Common Love Substitutes

<u>Charmers</u>

Your favorite line to her: *"Ain't I something?"*
Your favorite response from her: *"Wow! You really are
    something."*

Lloyd is attractive, but certainly not movie-star hand-some. He earns decent money, but is by no means living large. He's always perfectly groomed, impeccably dressed, and clearly possesses a polite, self-assured, highly charismatic manner that causes him to stand out. Lloyd comes across as refreshingly down-to-earth, a sensitive Southern gentleman who always appears to have it all together. His frat brothers all envy him and work hard to emulate his style. Women see Lloyd as a fascinating, generous, highly spiritual, and emotion-ally expressive man with no signs of the ego-driven, macho baggage that sisters often complain about in men. He lavishly performs every possible romantic detail, dazzling women with what seems to be a perfect blend of finesse and sincerity. In recent years, nearly two dozen women have phoned their mother and their closest sister-friends to rave about this "incredible brother called Lloyd, who just may be the one . . ."

But none of these women ever found out whether he was or wasn't. For in every case, in anywhere from three days to three months, Lloyd would "evaporate." He'd stop calling and returning calls, he'd stop sending those sweetly worded, handwritten notes, and he'd stop leaving those surprise single yellow roses on her windshield. As usual, charming Lloyd had appeared in an impressive flash of glory, then mysteriously ended up missing in action. And, as usual, he'd never be heard from again.

Gregory's sensitivity and extravagantly affectionate ways had swept Vanessa off her feet. It didn't take but a hot minute for him to start talking marriage. "Why not," thought Vanessa: Gregory was the most romantic and devoted man she'd ever met. Gregory really got into the whole wedding process. He was energized by making the plans and deciding the details of the grand-scale ceremony befitting royalty. Gregory felt like Prince Charming, and he knew how to make Vanessa feel like Cinderella. During the early months of their marriage, Gregory, intoxicated by passion for his awestruck bride, proved to be a generous provider, not to mention a sensational lover, with a flair for the dramatic. He took pains to make sure they had just the right house, the right car, the right clothes and vacations, all of which made them the most admired and envied couple in their circle.

Later, when the intense adrenaline rush of a new marriage with new experiences and lots of new stuff gave way to the normal, often uneventful, pace of day-to-day married life, Gregory's interest and enthusiasm began to wane. Eventually, painfully bored, restless, and claustrophobic, Prince Charming shocked Cinderella when "out of nowhere" he informed her that the ball was over and he wanted to move out of the palace.

Charmers live to impress. They believe maintaining their woman's undistracted attention and unending applause is what love is all about. Always seductive, a Charmer promises to exceed his woman's most idealistic romantic fantasies, no matter what the costs. Thrilling her is what thrills him and pumps up his sense of significance.

Underneath it all, Charmers look to women to decide their worth and value as men. They feel they must become her knight in shining armor. Only they can't afford for her to spot any cracks in that armor. He presents her a perfect picture of masculine greatness—goodness is not enough, only greatness will do. Charmers aren't at peace until their women say, "Wow!" That's why they are at their best during the early hyper-romantic stages of a relationship, when intensity is high and appearances can be carefully controlled. They repeatedly find relationships to be all quick-hot passion—yet superficial and temporary. Keeping up his perfect image and hiding his flaws from her scrutiny become increasingly difficult as a growing relationship requires more openness, substantive self-disclosure, and depth. To Charmers, that kind of intimacy soon feels too close for comfort. They work overtime to protect their sense of significance from the risks associated with her close examination of him, and the less-than-glorious estimation of him she could make. Charmers "check out," mentally, emotionally, and physically, *before* their women get a chance to see anything that could make them less than 100 percent in awe of him.

Charmers:

- Are image-obsessed and instinctively know how to construct and maintain an image that thoroughly impresses women.
- Constantly compare themselves with other men and are driven by a secret need to be more than other men (more romantic, more sensitive, more honest, more committed . . . more everything).

? • Think they truly desire close, committed relationships, when in fact they are commitment-phobic.
  • Don't withdraw out of a desire to hurt, exploit, or abandon women, but to protect themselves from the potential "dangers" of intimate long-term relationships.

Are You a Charmer?

True or false?

1. In the early stages of a new relationship (or at the start of a newly reconciled one), you use massive amounts of your time, your money, and your words to romance her, with the goal of "blowing her mind."

2. You brag to your male friends about how "hooked" she is on you and what you did to cause her to be.

3. You usually require a tremendous amount of prep time (for your clothes, car, hair, mood, and so forth) before you go out with her.

4. You tell little white lies, leave out facts, justify or keep secret things that don't cast you in your best light before her.

5. You feel a euphoric kind of high when your woman shows she is overwhelmed by your splendor.

6. You tend to be painfully bored in relationships after the conquest is over and you are married or otherwise officially committed to a Black woman.

7. Before you drift from a woman, you stop to figure out a justifiable reason for moving on, one that casts her in a negative light.

8. Though you tolerate it, you have to work hard to listen to her speak at length about herself. But it's no work at all to listen to her rave about you.

9. You seldom, if ever, maintain friendship on any level with a previous lover you've broken up with.

✓**10.** You have little patience with Black women who are emotionally reserved or stingy with their praise.

11. Though you work to cultivate many impressive qualities, there is one unique feature you have (your trademark) that you really love women (and even other men) to notice and admire.

12. The beginning, middle, and end of your relationships tend to have a distinct and often repeated pattern, with the way into and out of them seldom varying.

✓**13.** You are constantly trying to come up with new ways to make her more and more impressed with you.

14. You resent women's probing questions.

15. You have moved to break off a relationship even before you wanted to when you have sensed that she was about to do it first.

If you answered true to any of these, you could well have a bit of the Charmer in you. The more times you answered true, the more deeply ingrained and acceptable to you this significance-seeking love substitute has become, and the more it shows up in your style of relating to Black women.

All of the Policies and Procedures to come are for you, but especially those that have the ▲ symbol. Pay closest attention to them, because for you they are the most crucial—and the ones you are most likely to deny, resist, or ignore.

Your Dream Woman

She is the kind of flawless Black woman whom every man on the planet would love to have, but can't. She is utterly captivated by you and is extremely vocal about how much of a romancer you are. She spends her days approving, applauding, and standing in reverent awe of you. You spend your days working successfully to maintain the euphoric buzz that you get from creating new ways for her to see how fabulous you are.

Your Obstacle to Overcome

Self-obsession. You are so focused on what will make you look good, sound good, and—above all—feel good, you can't afford to care much about her for very long.

As You Read This Book

You will resent and take issue with criticism directed at you and your "charming" ways. You will work very hard to find the holes in my words and proof of how little you need to hear this. You'll think Black women are happy with your captivating style of loving. Taking constructive criticism and exerting effort to actually be (as opposed to merely appearing) more excellent seem just too tedious and uneventful. To you looking well is as good as being well. You could also be tempted to browse through the advice ahead simply to discover the "tricks" and "techniques" that could help you do even better at "wowing" women and manipulating their response to your image.

The action advice to come can be especially beneficial to Charmers, because it will provide you some concrete ways to work against your natural self-centeredness and relate to Black women with a fresh new priority on what they can get out of it. The beauty of it is when you begin to give for her sake, you'll end up on the getting end yourself. Your love could get some new discipline and therefore some new depth as well. You'll get to settle down and sample real-life, day-to-day love where two people get to accept, value, and remain committed to each other. And, most importantly, they will continue to, in spite of the fact that neither of them really is eternally extraordinary!

As you move through this book I highly recommend that you:

ADMIT that you possess Charmer tendencies. Your love substitute is one of the trickiest of them all when it comes to applying the Policies and Procedures. If you aren't honest with yourself you'll apply this advice with the same old tired motives—to create drama, to impress and to get standing ovations from the Black women in your life. If you continue that way you are sure to keep impressing them. And you are just as sure to keep experiencing quickie romances or an extremely hollow marriage.

RESIST the urge to decide the quality of the advice here and your response to it solely based on your feelings. Your feelings have not always led you to what is honorable, excellent, and important, but only to what boosts your ego and elevates your adrenaline.

EXPECT that by throwing off your performing ways and following the advice ahead you'll feel naked and less in control of the flow of the relationship, or of her perceptions of your greatness. Stay on the job anyway. It will eventually prove liberating for you to be able to stick around and not give in to fakeness or flight, or sacrifice another Black woman's hopes and emotions on the altar of your self-image.

COMMIT to allowing yourself some trial-and-error time as you apply the Policies and Procedures. Remember, you are working to gain more excellence in love—and not just to avoid the exposure of your imperfections. Reclaim from women the power you give them to define your worth based on their approval. Start from the belief that your worth and value are already established because of who you are, not because of the impressive things you do.

Improvers

Your favorite line to her: *"Why don't you just try my suggestion? I'm only trying to help."*
Your favorite response from her: *"Thanks. That's exactly what I'll do."*

There's only one thing that frustrates Phillip about Anita. It's that she has so much potential but sometimes won't let him show her how to develop it. Phillip feels that, among other things, her style of dress, the way she expresses herself, her career choices, and even her hairstyle (*especially* her hairstyle) are all things that he could dramatically improve if she would just listen. After all, he swears, he's only trying to help the woman he loves become all that she can be.

When he ended nearly thirty years of a rocky marriage to Doris, Melvin swore he'd never get involved with another Black woman. His experience was that they were way too stubborn and arrogant to deal with. It always irked Melvin that when he offered Doris his opinion or advice on a decision she had to make, she'd listen, thank him politely, then choose a completely different course of action than the one he had "suggested." Melvin couldn't bear Doris's ingratitude any longer.

Following a very brief courtship, Melvin married his secretary, Shanel, who was over twenty years his junior. Now here was a good woman who was willing to learn from her man, thought Melvin. Shanel was like a mound of clay ready and willing for him to mold into something exceptional. He knew he'd be good for her and, when he was finished making his improvements on her, she'd be good for him as well.

Both Phillip and Melvin are Improvers. They have very definite ideas as to what kind of woman they want and need. She is, of course, the kind who perfectly fits the image of himself he wants to project. She enhances his self-portrait by adding all her impressive glory to his. Improvers look for women who hold the promise of becoming an extension of his own identity. All in the name of love, he attempts to refurbish that woman into a perfect accessory to himself. Improvers don't know anymore where he ends and she begins. To them there is no you or me; there is only us.

Improvers "need" their women to listen up and willingly follow the blueprint they have designed for her. Love, to him, means caring enough about her to show her how he'd like her to be. He feels she should care enough about him to become it. An Improver has very exacting specifications and countless tools and techniques to rearrange, refurbish, or completely rebuild his woman into the image that he believes will get him applause and thus inflate his sense of significance.

Improvers mean their women no harm; they truly believe that they have their highest good in mind. They just know how rotten they can feel if the way their women come across is anything less than glorious perfection.

Improvers:

- Derive much of their sense of identity and significance from the external, observable things they do, possess, or are closely identified with, for example, their appearance, jobs, cars, homes, and especially their women.
- Are motivated by how others perceive them.
- Are creative, hardworking, and constantly on guard to protect, reframe, or enhance their image.
- Expect their women's love to be evidenced by their willingness to express his tastes and expectations, preferably without him having to ask them to.
- Use subtle forms of punishment (like silence, withdrawal, or guilt) to influence their women's willing participation in their improvement efforts.

• Try to convince their women and themselves that the opinions of others don't really matter to them.

Are You an Improver?

True or false?

1. At the last minute your woman's choice of attire can make you decide not to go to a social gathering that you had previously been looking forward to attending.
2. You have gotten far more offended and embarrassed by someone's minor criticism of your mate than she did.
3. You are aware that you have a subtle way of coaching her or correcting her behavior in public.
4. You try to use reverse psychology to get her to choose something your way, so that you can't be accused of being controlling.
5. You feel an intense need to clarify, make a joke of, or do other damage control when she has spoken or acted in a way that embarrassed you.
6. You have a vivid mental picture of the kind of woman you wish you were being seen with, instead of the one you have.
7. There are one or more specific features about her that you find glaringly deficient, and, try as you might, you can't help obsessing over it.
8. You rarely feel lasting contentment with your woman or with yourself.
9. The most significant conflict issues in your relationship have to do with control, personal rights, and acceptance.
10. You are known and respected for your superior taste, style, and creativity.
11. You often wish you were more relaxed and didn't care so much about other people's opinion of you.

12. You automatically give yourself a long mental performance review after you have interacted with someone you had hoped to impress.

13. Like a chameleon, you are seldom consistent in your personality or style from one place to another. You get annoyed when she doesn't shift her "role" to fit yours without your having to ask.

14. You constantly give reminders and repeat yourself when explaining your wishes and requests to her.

If you answered true to any of these you could well have a bit of the Improver in you. The more times you answered true, the more deeply ingrained and acceptable to you this significance-seeking love substitute has become, and the more it shows up in your style of relating to Black women.

All 70 of the Policies and Procedures to come are for you, but especially those that have the ◆ symbol. Pay closest attention to them, because for you they are the most crucial—and the ones you are most likely to deny, resist, or ignore.

Your Dream Woman

You've got a Black woman whose total being, personality, talents, communication style, visual presentation, and priorities perfectly reflect your taste and the image of yourself you have designed in your mind. You'd love her dearly because she'd be receptive to all your molding and shaping—and you wouldn't even have to hide it. She'll let you make her into a female version of you.

Your Obstacle to Overcome

Self-conscious insecurity. Your sense of significance is too much derived from other people's estimation of you. Fact is, you are the only one who is paying that much attention to you and to what your woman's image means about you. Never quite satisfied that either of you is turning out according to your plan, you can't seem to stop your compulsive improving.

As You Read This Book

The biggest challenge for you as you encounter the Policies and Procedures ahead will be heeding the advice when you can't immediately see how it will enhance, or at least maintain, that fully detailed self-image you have inside your head.

For you, expending effort, especially the hard effort needed to effect change, is only worth it when you can clearly and promptly help your world, and everything in it, rise to your soaring levels of expectation. You only feel truly safe from being looked down upon, ridiculed, or embarrassed when you've managed to put all costumes, props, and scenery in place. You have little time left to meet her needs and nourish her life.

You drive women crazy trying to manipulate them into giving up their way of being, in order to adopt yours. Their sense of security can't flourish in the chilly climate of your discontent. You stay too tense and you make the people around you tense, because it's clear: Enough is *never* enough for you. Your constant subtle requests and your cleverly disguised rewards-and-punishment system, combined with that "well, forget you then" attitude of yours, make it nearly impossible for a sister to know that you absolutely treasure her just as she is.

An Improver gives his woman only one acceptable way of nurturing his significance—willing cooperation with his never-ending efforts to use her to "decorate" himself. It's a price that few Black women are willing to pay for very long. The paradox is that the ones who will let themselves be shaped on your wheel and molded in your image will still have a hard time getting your lasting commitment. Because when it's all said and done, Improvers are turned off by women who "need" so much improving in the first place!

Much of what you will read here about what is truly important to Black women (and not merely get from them for the sake of your image) will be hard for you to buy into. You've encountered women who'd be happy to be your fix-it project and are grateful for the opportunity. This, you may well argue, is proof that "improving" *is* your way of loving, and it *is* beneficial to her, and it would be senseless to change now.

But it is vital that you change. If you don't, the trail of Black women who have been manipulated to conform to your secret designs, or those who have been rejected and insulted by your demanding requirements, will only get longer. And your disillusionment and distaste for your woman, or *all* Black women, will only increase.

Your challenge to change requires that you:

ADMIT that the Improver drive in you has failed you miserably. You are neither giving nor getting the kind of others-centered, mutually satisfying love that you want. You must confront the part of you which believes that image is everything. You'll savor the peace that comes from leaving the land of Me, Myself, and I.

RESIST the urge to elevate yourself above the advice found ahead. Since your constant self-appraisal seldom leaves you satisfied with your woman or yourself, you have a tendency to compensate by pretending superiority. That kind of pride-filled self-perception will only keep you doing it your old Improver way. Just think of yourself as one of us: a man who needs more than his own design to become all he should become. You could use some designs to live by that you didn't create and that aren't just for your benefit.

EXPECT an inclination in you, as you work to follow the advice, to look for a "tit for tat" arrangement with your woman. If you start to perform these nice, new security-nurturing things for her, you could require her to pay you back before you proceed to do more. But that's just more of the same old trick you have fallen prey to, too many times as it is. Now's the time to give up your bargaining, swapping, and bartering policy and begin to do things for her in clear, direct, positive ways that result in a benefit to her. From now on work to do right by her—because it's right to do, not because it pays.

COMMIT to letting go of your rigid, albeit subtly demanded, requirements of her, and the cold shoulder you give when she doesn't comply. Refuse to allow your will to follow your feelings, once again, down the road of obsession over how you are being perceived. Simply decide that for now the Black woman you love is good enough as she is, and she doesn't owe you any improvements.

Blamers

Your favorite line to her: *"It's all your fault!"*
Your favorite response from her: *"You are so right. I'm sorry."*

Nothing drives Kirk crazier than when his wife, Denise, starts insisting that they should see a marriage counselor. She always brings up what she calls their "total breakdown of communication," their strained feelings about their tight finances, and her frustration over not being able to get pregnant. It all sounds to Kirk like his wife is trying to lay all the blame on him. He loudly insists that if Denise would just grow up and stop dwelling on the negatives there wouldn't be any problems that require throwing good money away on some nosy counselor.

Stephan pulled the plug very abruptly on his long-distance romance with Alicia. He concluded that she obviously was not the Black woman for him, after she tearfully expressed her disappointment that he had failed to call, mail a card, or in any way acknowledge her recent birthday. In fact, Alicia was still upset about Stephan's having broken his promise to fly into her city and spend Valentine's weekend with her. After all, she noted, it was his idea in the first place! Stephan felt that there was no way Alicia could be the one for him if she didn't have enough insight to understand these circumstances were not really his fault. A man gets busy and things do come up. Besides, Stephan reasoned, Alicia's fault-finding attitude was a much more serious and destructive problem than any "totally unintentional" mistakes he may have made.

Blamers are the ultimate finger-pointers. They can't bear the possibility that any of the problems or challenges to intimacy in their relationships could ever, in any way, be their fault. To hear him tell it, he's *never* to blame and therefore he never has to assume the burden of accountability and change. Blaming her, "the system," the world, "them," "things," or virtually anything other than himself is what keeps him from having to assume responsibility. And, if he wasn't responsible, then no one can ever say he failed. And never seeming to have failed is how he keeps a tight hold on his cherished sense of significance.

Blamers:

- Have 20/20 vision when it comes to the imperfections of others. They fake blindness when it comes to their own imperfections.

- Possess a built-in "risk-radar." They instinctively avoid at the outset, or later disassociate themselves from, people, places, or pursuits that might make them vulnerable to real or perceived failure. (This is especially true in love relationships.)
- Can't help interpreting their woman's negative feelings or experiences about anything as accusations against him.
- Are perpetually angry and disappointed over what the Black woman in his life does or doesn't do.
- Are skilled masters in the art of self-justification, defensiveness, and rationalization.
- Only experience one-sided relationships where improvement, correction, responsibility, apologies, and vulnerability are her stuff, not his.

Are You a Blamer?

True or false?

1. More than one of the women in your life have accused you of "turning things around to make yourself look innocent."
2. You get uncomfortable when your woman is upset. You don't get comfortable again until she makes it clear she's not blaming you for her problem.
3. You "script" handy excuses and explanations in your mind for future use with your woman, and you keep a readily available mental file of her faults and shortcomings.
4. In heated conflict with your mate you habitually use statements like "Yeah, but what about you . . ." or "At least I'm being honest about what I did, but you . . ." or "The real problem is not about me, it's how you . . ."

5. When you explain your relationship difficulties to others you revise the events or put a spin on your motives that makes you more innocent and her more guilty.

6. You deeply resent anyone (particularly your woman) having a complaint in a given area, especially if you feel you've performed extraordinarily in some other area of your relationship.

7. You employ creative ways to fish for compliments or head off blame.

8. You absolutely love to be apologized to.

9. You have surprised yourself by how violent your feelings and how intense your outbursts are when you are accused of a wrong by your woman.

10. Most people in your life find you far more genteel, charming, and fair-minded than your woman does.

11. At times you have been excessively concerned with who she talks to about the two of you and have gone out of your way to clear your good name.

12. The women in your life whom you have felt strongest about and remained longest with aren't nearly as quick-witted, articulate, insightful, or demanding as you.

13. You believe that usually, when women complain about you, it's because they are the kind who are irrational, judgmental, and unwilling to face their own defects.

If you answered true to any of these you could well have a bit of the Blamer in you. The more times you answered true, the more deeply ingrained and acceptable to you this significance-seeking love substitute has become, and the more it shows up in your style of relating to Black women.

All 70 of the Policies and Procedures to come are for you, but especially those that have the ● symbol. Pay closest attention to them, because for you they are the most crucial—and the ones you are most likely to deny, resist, or ignore.

Your Dream Woman

She's a low-maintenance, high-performance Black woman who feels fortunate to have a man like you. She's only aware of your admirable qualities and never even notices that you have bad ones. As far as she is concerned you're perfect and she is humble and honest enough to realize that if something does go wrong it must be her fault—or anybody's fault— except yours.

Your Obstacle to Overcome

The compulsive need to be right. It's how you get your applause. Blamers secretly struggle with guilt and disappointment with themselves. They are supremely legalistic. If you are a Blamer, you really don't believe you are perfect and guiltless—you believe it takes flawless performance to be a good (not even a perfect) man. In spite of all appearances, your self-confidence level runs at a deficit. Any blame, criticism, or disapproval indicates to you that you are even less than you thought you were. Therefore you can't ever afford to be wrong. Total self-righteousness is the key to maintaining your sense of significance.

As You Read This Book

It could be a real effort for you to continue further in this book at all. Blamers have a way of filtering advice, and the challenge to change, that makes it all sound to them like shaming rebukes and condemnation—the very stuff you're most allergic to. And if you make it to the Policies and Procedures ahead and decide to try them, they could overwhelm you because of your inner compulsion to do everything perfectly, right now, or not try to do it at all. With that mind-set, this book could be dangerous to your mental health—unless you insist that your self-sabotaging mind-set sit down and shut up, then proceed to act in direct opposition to it.

The fact of the matter is, *nobody* in your life except you requires you to be 100 percent blame-free. Most people, and that's likely to include your woman, only want you to own up to your mess and make and keep a commitment to fix it. You may have a hard time believing it, but your woman would rather see your warts and flaws and know you care enough about her and yourself to work on them, than for you to have no faults or failures or blame in the first place. Few people, and none that you should want to be bothered with, toss someone aside simply because they are imperfect but are working toward becoming better.

As you take the steps recommended ahead, virtually everything can be different for you and your mate if you give up hiding, displacing, or ignoring your flaws. Become willing to let them see the light of day. You are keeping yourself so safely protected by your blaming that your woman doesn't get to intimately know huge parts of you. It's like making love with an elegant cashmere overcoat on.

Of course, sometimes you really won't be at fault, and she will. Sometimes you will be falsely accused and unjustly treated. You needn't deny the truth in order to change your ways. It's just that your impassioned crusade, and the way you work over-time to exonerate yourself, make you too much the crafty defense attorney. It has become an oppressive chore, for you, and the worst kind of insult to her.

If you are willing to give up your preoccupation with self-protection in the name of significance, you and the Black woman you love can powerfully benefit from the Policies and Procedures in Part II. You can start by taking the following steps now:

ADMIT that you are a Blamer (or that you, at least, carry some of those traits in your system). Go ahead and acknowledge that it has cost you and the woman in your life way too much already. You won't get anywhere near the more balanced, honest, and fulfilling life and relationship you want if you keep using your "yeah buts . . ." to squirm out of facing the truth head-on.

RESIST that impulse to focus on the Policies and Procedures that you feel you already do well and ignore the ones that challenge you to advance beyond the borders of your comfort zone. You'll need to be ready to do what *doesn't* come naturally—and what could expose some of your weak spots. You'll discover it won't kill you, it'll change you—and for the better.

EXPECT to struggle with the notion that your woman doesn't deserve all these caring, securing behaviors. You may think she sees your kindness as weakness. Remember your old misbelief system is based on the idea that one only deserves good who always does good. Your well-reinforced self-protective strategies have worked hard to convince you that she certainly hasn't earned it. In fact, you have now bought into the idea that all those faults you have projected onto her are somehow true and she *is* at fault. In spite of this legalistic, earned-rewards system, you need practice at giving grace (unearned favor) to her. It'll help you eventually learn to give some to yourself—where it's most needed.

COMMIT to putting these principles into practice, in spite of how messy, awkward, and chaotic it may initially feel. Go ahead and feel all those unsettling feelings—just don't follow them. They'll only lead you back to seeking your significance through the deceptive appearance of perfection.

Givers

Your favorite line to her: *"Just tell me what you want and
I'll do it."*
Your favorite response from her: *"You are the sweetest man
on earth."*

As a boy, Calvin noticed the way the men in his family
treated their women. His father, assorted cousins, uncles, and
older brothers often bragged about how much their women
did for them and how little they had to do to get them to.
Calvin didn't understand it all, at the time, but he did find it
strange that the men seemed very proud to describe themselves as "players," "Mack Daddies," and "gigolos," while the
women referred to them as "good for nothing" or "not worth
a dime." Calvin saw the pain and dissatisfaction in his mother
and the others, and was determined to grow up and become,
in the eyes of his woman, a truly "extraordinary man,"
because to him:

- Ordinary men are selfish, egotistical, and insensitive to
  their women.
- Ordinary men exploit and mistreat their women.
- Ordinary men don't have a clue about the fine points of
  a woman's needs and desires, let alone what it takes to
  fulfill them.
- Ordinary men end up with women who hate them and
  regret ever having gotten involved with their kind.

All grown up now, Calvin tends to go way overboard trying to prove to the Black woman he loves that he's definitely
not one of those good-for-nothing men. His policy is to guess,
ask, assume, or imagine what his woman desires and do

whatever he's got to do to deliver it, ASAP. Women start out seeing Calvin as the sweetest, most attentive, and caring man. Later they call him a spineless jellyfish who can only be counted on to make all kinds of promises and seldom make good on them. They swear he set them up by being so unusually attentive and generous at first, then, stubbornly, abruptly stopping—*and*, mysteriously, refusing to explain why.

Antonio thought himself unbelievably lucky to have landed an absolute goddess, like Regina, as his wife. Regina was in a class by herself, miles beyond the colorless, easily pleased women he was accustomed to.

As if to somehow make up for the callous insensitivity he had shown Black women in the past, Antonio went out of his way for Regina. He found her to be so much more *everything*: more beautiful, more popular, more successful and pulled together than any woman he could have ever expected to have. Regina was a thoroughbred, through and through. And if she was a little spoiled, demanding, and nitpicky, thoroughbreds are just a high-maintenance breed, Antonio reasoned. He was so honored to have Regina he made sure to do (or at least appear to do) whatever he thought the lady wanted, with no complaints and no delays. Though he never would admit it, his friends were convinced Antonio's nose was wide open.

Later, Antonio became aware of having mixed emotions about Regina. On the one hand, he was sick and tired of bowing and scraping, overspending, predicting her needs, and biting his tongue. Antonio began to lose respect for himself and to despise Regina for the power he felt she had over him. But, on the other hand, he worshipped her, and craved her presence in his life. There was no way he was going to give her up, or the intoxicating sense of significance her approval brought.

Over time Antonio constructed, layer by layer, a secret world of well-concealed activities, debts, and extramarital relationships. Much of his life was a complete mystery to everyone—including his wife. He found clever, indirect ways of getting back at Regina, without her being able to pin anything on him with any assurance.

Givers are generous, agreeable, and self-sacrificing "servants" who maintain their sense of significance in relationships with Black women they idolize by guessing and satisfying every need, whim, or expectation he even thinks she has. Givers gain their significance by packaging themselves as humble, benevolent men who only live to serve their women. They ask for little and are willing to give everything—except the emotional goodies their women crave, like: direct, unambiguous commitments, integrity, and enough self-respect and assertiveness to say what they really mean and mean what they say—even when NO is what they really mean.

Givers have looked around at the blatantly uncaring and disrespectful manner in which some men relate to Black women and they've listened when the women have expressed hurt and anger about their relationships with men. Givers covet the chance to appear to be that rare, sensitive hero who is everything those other bums aren't. If you're a Giver, manipulating the way things appear is your strong suit. "Have no fear," you'll vow to her, "I'm only here to give, not to take."

But Givers have a big secret: They don't give and give for her sake—they do it for themselves, in order to keep what they feel they need: the sense of peerless virtue and power they gain from their own ceaseless benevolence and the warm glow of their woman's approval. They exalt Black women to a level approaching worship, where disappointing her is not an option—at least not at first. With all his lavish, tender loving care, a Giver usually succeeds at making his woman feel cherished and secure—only to eventually pull the rug right out from under her when she least expects it.

All this work and worship always leaves the Giver feeling:

- *Torn.* You do get a measure of self-satisfaction from presenting yourself as such a wonderfully caring man. But you hate yourself for compromising and for feeling so approval-needy. You want to be free of this, but you don't want to lose her.
- *Worn.* The more you overdo in order to keep her happy and ensure her approval, the more commonplace (i.e., not at all extraordinary) your offerings become, the more giving or guessing or predicting you must do in order to be seen as an exceptional man.
- *Forlorn.* When being your outrageously over-the-top version of a "really nice guy" begins to register to you as self-compromising and one-sided you are likely to retreat to a secret world where you get to be the opposite of how you are with her. As your secret world gets more of your attention and your real life and relationships gets less, your deceptions, mysterious behaviors, and the massive losses you are willing to incur ignite a sense of shame in you.

Are You a Giver?

True or false?

1. You put almost all your energy into finding out what your woman expects and little to none into clearly expressing what you want and expect.

2. You have experienced overwhelming guilt, on more than a few occasions, when she expressed disappointment with something you failed to do.

3. You have some ongoing secret activities, relationships, or major problem (related to your finances, your health, your possessions, or your career) that you work extremely hard to keep her from knowing the complete truth about.

✓**4.** You love it when your woman makes dramatic comparisons between your exceptional goodness and other men's no-goodness.

5. You would be more than a little embarrassed if your male friends found out the extent to which you work to please your woman, and some of the inappropriate treatment you've accepted from her without a word.

6. You have gotten a secret jolt of satisfaction when something very important to her fell apart and it could, in no way, be pinned on you.

7. When you are angry with her, you sometimes intentionally procrastinate, ignore, or "forget" commitments made to her.

✓**8.** You tend to avoid conflicts and the emotionalism that accompanies them, and are quick to assume responsibility for making the conflict go away.

9. You typically start out exceptionally romantic, creative, and generous in your gift-giving, downshifting later to perfunctory gift-giving and "as required" expressions of affection.

✓**10.** You will lie, exaggerate, or otherwise alter the facts if you think it will keep the peace or protect yourself from her finding out you messed up.

11. Though you deny it, you have strategically withheld sex to punish her or to make a point.

12. You hold grudges and seldom forget a slight or a criticism, continuing to replay them in your mind.

13. You have reacted to her ultimatums with either extreme apologies and extravagant promises or outright begging.
14. Though you hate it, you have also envied the relative ease with which your woman can do without you.
15. On at least one occasion you have lost control and gotten physical with your mate.
16. At least one Black woman has broken off with you claiming that your lack of assertiveness, irresponsibility, and secretiveness were real turn-offs.

If you answered true to any of these, you could well have a bit of the Giver in you. The more times you answered true, the more deeply ingrained and acceptable to you this significance-seeking love substitute has become, and the more it shows up in your style of relating to Black women.

All of the Policies and Procedures to come are for you, but especially those that have the ❱ symbol. Pay closest attention to them, because for you they are the most crucial—and the ones you are most likely to deny, resist, or ignore.

Your Dream Woman

She's the world's most exceptional and admired woman who has already been with the world's most horrible men. Rejecting the multitudes of hopeless "bad boys" she picks you. Because with all your exceptional sincerity, sensitivity, and generosity she recognizes that you are nothing like them. She never requires any more from you than what you already give. To her, you will be forever extraordinary.

Your Obstacle to Overcome

The fear of losing out. Your overgiving and passivity cost you your self-respect. But you are afraid that if you stop, or take the necessary steps to bring some balance and limits to what you give to her and take from her, you could lose her and the sense of significance you derive from being seen as exceptional in her eyes.

As You Read This Book

If you're not careful, in your hands, this book could be lethal. Since you are already so deeply invested in woman-pleasing you might be inclined to use the advice found here to help you do it more and better. You'll immediately latch on to the directives that call upon a man's humility and self-sacrificing. You'll skip right over those that challenge you to stand up for yourself, set limits, tell the truth, and be willing to endure some losses.

Just pages from now, you really might be tempted to close this book, shelve it, and go away arguing that this is only good medicine for bad men, and you'll convince yourself that you are such an exemplary fellow already you need none of what's prescribed here. That'll be your cue to go right back to the sweat-soaked song and dance your love life has become and try to escape back to your secret life.

But it really doesn't have to be this way. Your approach to love, self-respect, and the needed sense of significance can be radically transformed by acquiring new motives and new, healthier ways of relating to the Black woman you love. When you stop being so driven by the fear of losing her, to your "please her at any cost" tendencies, you can become a much more balanced and honest man. One who gives because he can and because he wants to. And you'll rightly expect her to give to you as well, because you deserve it no less than she does.

To make that vital transformation you will need to:

ADMIT that you are a Giver and that what you have been

doing for the woman you love has proven, in the long run, not to benefit either of you. If you're honest, you will admit that it has eventually made you both have little respect for you. Don't confuse the terms, your kind of giving is not caring sacrifice, unconditional love, or exceptional devotion. It's people-pleasing—pure giving in order to get!

RESIST the urge to use the advice in the next section as merely different ways to do the same old stuff for the same old reasons. The Policies and Procedures ahead are to empower you to be appropriately responsive to her needs as well as to your own. They are *not* tips on how take complete responsibility for her life.

EXPECT the scalpel to cut deeply as you work to surgically remove the malignant self-centeredness at your core. A sense of guilt and ambivalence about changing your style may tempt you to abort the process. Don't. Even if, as you begin to show signs of changing, your woman accuses you of becoming "just like all those other dogs," you *must* stay on-task. Change is traumatic for everyone, even those who could benefit most from your transformation. You'll learn to live with her temporary displeasure and the self-doubts they stir in you, by keeping to your goals. You'll discover that your worst fear—her disapproval—may hurt, but it won't kill you. And, when it stops having such a powerful hold on you, you'll have no use for your old self-sabotaging love substitute.

COMMIT, throughout the entire process (i.e., the rest of your life), to learning to say no (literally, and loudly) to yourself when you are tempted to say and do things solely to earn her love and her willingness to be with you. Instead, freely offer her the mutually beneficial Policies and Procedures upcoming. It's a trickier task than you might imagine. Having a buddy who has your permission to probe your motives and question your behavior will prove to be an invaluable asset as you apply the principles ahead.

Rulers

Your favorite line to her: *"I am the man here, you know."*
Your favorite response from her: *"Yes, you are the man."*

Curtis was one of the most eligible and sought-after bachelors at his church. A former pro football player turned businessman, he was tall, broad-shouldered, and possessed an intense, no-nonsense demeanor that was both attractive and off-putting to women. Curtis was a thoroughly imposing figure around whom most people felt they were expected to do more listening than talking.

In spite of the fact that Curtis had gone through the church's premarital counseling program for engaged couples three times—with three different women—finding a good Christian woman to be his loving and submissive wife was beginning to seem like a next-to-impossible challenge for him.

Curtis was convinced that the average Black woman was no longer willing to submit to what he believed was a man's God-given right to rule over her. Curtis frequently complained about how each of his mates eventually showed their true colors when they "challenged my authority and tried to be the man in the relationship." Curtis believed that for a marriage to work, his job was to command with absolute, but loving, power. Her job was to defer her ideas, opinions, and expertise and follow his dictates to the letter—and enjoy doing it too!

Jamal's favorite affectionate pet name for his girlfriend Donna was "Daddy's Baby Girl." Though they'd been together only six months, Jamal took great pride in the degree of respect shown him by Donna. He had no problem seeing to her rent, her car note, and giving her a weekly allowance for her kids. How could he complain, he figured. Here was a woman who called him "Daddy" and treated him like a king. She never made the slightest decision without Jamal signing off on it, and she apologized profusely whenever she "talked back" to him and "made him" have to slap her one. In Jamal's mind Donna was a very lucky girl to have a man like him to take care of her.

Rulers are dictators who have granted themselves all rights to the throne in their relationships with Black women. If you are a ruler, you maintain your sense of significance by your authoritative, paternal, and ultimately condescending style of relating to women. Deep down you believe that being a "real man" means being in charge, and you believe that women, bless their hearts, really need you to be. Therefore Rulers of every kind, from the most well bred and mild-mannered to the most raving megalomaniacs, believe that it is in their woman's best interest that he be in control, so he expects her willing submission to his lordship. Ruling can seem like a brand-new lease on life if you have felt put down, dismissed, or "worked over" by some mean-spirited, domineering female only out to reduce a brother to dust.

Rulers employ every conceivable means to rise to power and then to maintain it and the significance jolt that comes with it. At every turn they must draw upon their considerable talents as demanding bosses, convincing liars, frightful intimidators, knowledgeable instructors, insightful psychologists, or pouting, little boys to compel their women to accept and appreciate their man's rule.

At the core of Rulers' feelings of entitlement is the self-applied pressure to know all, be all, and make sure that all turns out according to their own predesigned plans. Rulers are big on getting results.

That's why they don't feel they can afford to share much of the power. They suspect that if they don't run things, then they can't be sure that all will proceed toward the results they have envisioned. If you're a Ruler, that's a tragedy of epic proportions, because you need *your* results to get the credit, the applause, and the feelings of significance you yearn for.

Of course, being a Ruler has some extraordinary costs associated with it. Not the least of them has to do with how utterly disregarded and disrespected the women in your life tend to feel. No matter what you say, she knows she only gets to play a bit part, while you have the starring role in the drama that your relationship is. The Black women in your life eventually conclude that you care far less about them, and their security needs, than you care about yourself and what makes you feel significant.

Maybe you can begin to see why the women in your life don't just pack up and politely go, they go with a vengeance, wishing you the worst and delighting in your downfall. Or they stay, too tired or too afraid to pull the plug, but too hurt and angry to keep submitting to your tyranny. They remain with a hardened veneer over their dry indifference to you, your rulership, and your results.

Rather than taking this as a hint that you should consider sharing the throne, you only end up respecting Black women even less, seeing them as overaggressive male-bashers who aren't ready to be loved. The cycle continues because you'll feel the need to rule more firmly and allow for less dissent in your present relationship or your next one. You'll hurt more Black women's sense of security, and their negative responses will diminish your sense of significance, and the two of you will continue to make major contributions to each other's misery.

Rulers:

- Get an elevated sense of self-importance when their woman takes their words, wishes, and whims as her marching orders.

- Believe that the strength of their masculinity assures them of the right to rule, and that the frailty of her femininity necessitates her need to be ruled.
- Are convinced that their sovereignty greatly benefits their mate. But they tend to be suspicious of Black women's motives and deeply resent any rivalry, second-guessing, or "disobedience" from her.

Are You a Ruler?

True or false?

1. You have felt justified in spying, eavesdropping, or in some way monitoring your woman's activities.
2. Apologies are hard for you to formulate. You almost never just plain say, "I'm sorry, I was wrong."
3. You often use phrases like "You just don't understand . . ." when your woman objects to your ruling.
4. You are quick to make mental note of other men's leadership style and degree of authority and compare yourself to them.
5. You constantly reiterate the list of benefits your woman has derived from your being in charge.
6. You are a master of the silent treatment.
7. You have a very hard time when your mate wins or outdoes you at some competition, such as cards, or any contest or shared goal.
8. You have committed a harmful or illegal act in retaliation against a Black woman who crossed you.
9. You have few, if any, male friends who know about all the areas of your life.
10. You are prone to challenging authority figures—subtly or overtly.

11. You tell and highly enjoy jokes that make fun of women.

12. It is especially hard for you to contain your anger when your woman doesn't do something she's agreed to do or doesn't do it right.

13. You'd much prefer your woman obey you because she perceives it as benefiting her, not just you.

14. There is at least one Black woman, when you think of her, you get knots in your stomach and intensely angry feelings.

15. You lavishly reward your woman when she submissively complies with your wishes.

If you answered true to any of these you could well have a bit of the Ruler in you. The more times you answered true, the more deeply ingrained and acceptable to you this significance-seeking love substitute has become, and the more it shows up in your style of relating to Black women.

All of the Policies and Procedures to come are for you, but especially those that have the ■ symbol. Pay closest attention to them, because for you they are the most crucial—and the ones you are most likely to deny, resist, or ignore.

Your Dream Woman

She has a huge amount of confidence in you—but not in herself. She is highly verbal and extremely articulate—but only when she's talking about how powerful and brilliant you are. She's a genius—at least when it comes to understanding that, without you, her life would be so much less than it is.

Your Obstacle to Overcome

The addiction to control. Because men in our culture are often taught from childhood that he who is most man is he who is most in charge, ruling could well be called the significance jackpot. Rulers fear they'll fail to satisfy the minimum standards of masculinity if they don't maintain authoritarian control. Deep on the inside they suspect that something isn't quite right with their heavy-handed approach, but they feel certain they'll lose too much by yielding even an inch.

As You Read This Book

As a Ruler, you are likely to already be nursing the suspicion that this book, and especially the upcoming Policies and Procedures, will prove to be yet another discussion of how rotten Black men are and how mistreated Black women are. Even now you stand ready to shoot holes in the advice ahead because you are sure it doesn't take into account what you see as the absolute necessity of a strong Black man taking a firm hand of rulership in dealing with today's Black woman.

Your greatest temptation as you proceed through these pages will be to only scan the titles, subheadings, and highlighted words and phrases that, when lifted out of context, might help you build a strong case against the advice in the next section of this book. I caution you to be on the alert. There is likely to be momentum inside you propelling you away from taking ownership of the very information that most applies to you. Rulers will instinctively try to sidestep the principles here that have the most potential to transform their rigid, authoritarian love substitute into a strong yet compassionate, sure-of-yourself but yielding kind of love. It is that kind of love that the women in your life have long sought from you. It is love that is not so easily offended or intimidated by the force of her personality, her differences, her priorities, her opinions, and the way in which she expresses them. It's a love that has no problem listening, caring, or compromising, or even completely yielding at times.

Push through the upcoming pages, relying more on your open mind and listening ears than your debating tongue. Sure, you *have* paid the cost to be the boss; but look at the price you've paid. It has made women fear you, despise you, or cling like little girls to their Daddy's knee. And it has reduced your romantic relationship to something very close to an employer-employee one, with little trust or satisfying love flowing in either direction.

Changing your style, for your sake and hers, can happen if you will:

ADMIT that you have definite Ruler tendencies. With your passion for results, you need some compelling motivation to be able to vigorously pursue anything to successful completion. It's especially important for you that you see ruling for what it is, a self-sabotaging love substitute—and that you have been honest enough to see yourself as a man who has used it. When that realization makes you even a little sick and tired, you are ripe and ready to move toward change.

RESIST, for now, your constant attempts to enforce your authority with Black women, or to require her to do anything your way. Determine instead that now is the time to put your self-serving ways on indefinite hold and choose rather to serve your woman by practicing the powerful, but loving, actions suggested ahead.

EXPECT to feel as if you have "wimped out" and that you are now committing to do what you dread more than anything in the world: following someone else's rules. Don't believe it. For you to do what's suggested ahead will be because you have exercised your willful choice and have made a deliberate decision to act in new and more mutually rewarding ways.

COMMIT to allowing yourself time, maybe even a long time, to make the transition from a man who gets his significance from ruling to one who already has his significance and therefore is free to serve and to take pride in how effectively he does. In other words, don't rush so fast to the results stage that you minimize the importance of trial and error, slow but steady movement, and accepting your and your mate's best along the way.

Slow Down . . .
Men at Work!

By now I'm sure it's clear to you that this book is about how to do *The Job:* relating to the Black woman you love with the kind of skill and sensitivity that makes for mutual satisfaction. You really want her to feel satisfied with your love, but you also want to feel satisfied with yourself, and your ability to do the job well. Satisfying her and yourself are both priority one. To aim for either of them alone, and not the two of them together, is out of balance, unrealistic, and makes the prospect of accepting the job far less attractive.

Your summary job description does *not* read: *"Position involves finding out how Black women approach love and relationships and attempting to imitate them."* That's no help to anybody. That's definitely not the job.

Rather, it's about how to offer her the very best kind of love that fits her unique, legitimate needs in the very best ways you possibly can.

You needn't feel any shame over thinking about the way you express your love to her as a job. Often women, whose orientation to love is more abstract and feelings-based, misread your concrete, task-oriented approach as something less wholehearted and therefore less valid. Actually, the things men place the highest value on in life, we approach as a job to do, with goals and objectives, roles and responsibilities—and clearly detailed policies and procedures.

A more accurate summary job description for men in love could read:

Position involves loving a Black woman by:

- maintaining a constant focus on her high-priority need for security,
- striving to accurately "translate" her female communication style,
- choosing to speak when you'd much rather act, and
- keeping an open mind and heart willing to accept the vast differences between her style and yours.

Previous experience is not a requirement, but an unwavering commitment to serve your woman without either over- or undervaluing yourself is vital to your success.

The pages ahead contain seventy straightforward, sometimes challenging, but highly effective ways to love a Black woman. Some of what you will find may seem like "old news," and you'll be very proud of how well you already know and do them. Give them your attention anyway, as they will be useful reminders, helping you to troubleshoot and tighten up your weak areas and blind spots. Then keep reading and you will encounter others that will speak directly to you and your situation, challenging you to live out what is truly effective in loving a Black woman, with more wisdom, more courage, and ultimately, more genuine satisfaction for both of you.

Don't just analyze these Policies and Procedures—perform them. The most effective way to break old useless habits is to replace them with new, more effective ones. These can radically alter the way you and the woman in your life experience love. To adopt even a few of the directives ahead will make a dramatic difference in your life. To adopt most, or all, of them will revolutionize your relationship and, not coincidentally, transform you personally as well.

The Policies and Procedures and You

Give yourself time to carefully read and digest the insights and suggestions given for each of the Policies and Procedures. Pay closest attention to the ones that have your love substitute's symbol at the top of the page.

A brief personal statement "From the Black woman you love" precedes each of these seventy actions. None of them are the exact words of any one woman. The statements are, however, typical of what Black women have shared with me in private counseling, on talk shows, and at seminars around the country. This book is a "translation" in the male language of what women have wanted us to understand about what they need from us. In that they have often conveyed it to us in the female language, we haven't always gotten it. We've ended up filling in the gaps the best we know how.

At the end of each of the Policies and Procedures is an important section called "The Bottom Line" with three essential features. "Men at Work" will help you turn the principles into practice suggesting clear-cut, doable action responses to the insights you have just read. As you know, developing new skills and sharpening old ones require taking bold steps, not just reading about them.

Also included under each "Bottom Line" is a pair of concise statements that answer the two vital questions that are uppermost in a man's mind *before* he'll fully commit to a new task: (a) "If I do this, what are 'The Benefits' I can expect?" and (b) "What are 'The Costs' to get them?"

In every case you will notice that the benefits always outweigh even the most considerable costs.

You have now come to the point in reading this book that separates the proverbial men from the boys. It will, of course, take next to no energy or effort to turn the page here, in the literal sense. But the big question is: Are you now willing to rise to the challenge of turning a new page in your life and in your relationship with Black women?

The advice ahead is not a magic formula. It doesn't come with an unconditional guarantee. Love involves another human being, and wherever there is another human being involved in anything, there are no guarantees because you don't have control over the other person. Influence perhaps, maybe even powerful influence, but never control.

You do have control over yourself. Obviously, you don't have to do a thing you don't want to do. Nobody, not the woman in your life or anyone else, can force you to live what you'll learn here. There's not enough guilt, complaining, or ridicule in the world to make that happen. It's your choice. And if you decide to take the advice, it will be because *you* see Black women as worth it and *you* see yourself as able to do it. In both points, I wholeheartedly agree with you.

Life-changing possibilities do exist, just ahead, for you and for the woman you love. If you've chosen to accept the challenge, now is the time to roll up your sleeves and get down to business. The job—and the genuine satisfaction of doing it well—awaits you.

PART II

How to Love a Black Woman

1. ▲ ■ ● ◆ ◗
Reality-Check Your Expectations of Her

To the man who loves me:
I'm beginning to get the impression that you are judging me
when you look me over from head to toe and as you listen
intently when I am speaking to you or as you so carefully
check out the things I do and how I do them. I'm wondering
if you're looking to see if I measure up—and I'm wondering
what it is that I have to measure up to.

—From the Black woman you love

The hardest part of living real life is accepting the realities we find there. Even if you've never shared it with another living soul, somewhere in the secret recesses of your mind you probably have imagined your Ms. Right and how incredible she'd be in nearly every way. You've seen the way her flowing locks beautifully framed her face or dramatically draped her shoulders. You've heard her at her most delicately soft-spoken or sassily outspoken and you know to the smallest detail of her personality, her level of ambition, and the spiritual depth, passion, style, and humor she possesses. As far as you're concerned she's perfection personified and she's all yours. That is, once you ever find her. I hate to rain on your parade, but unless you reality-check your expectations, the Black woman you seek will never appear or the Black woman you have will never measure up.

Unrealistic expectations set you up for too much disappointment and make the women around you at risk for too much painful rejection. Keep your high hopes and high standards but by all means get rid of those self-sabotaging fantasies of a perfect Ms. Right. If there really is such a thing, she has already been taken by a Mr. Right!

In real-life relationships the man who loves a Black woman does well to reality-check his own perceptions and expectations of her from time to time. You must be brutally honest in answering these questions: Is what I am expecting of the woman in my life based on reality or merely wishes, fantasies, and daydreams? Is it mostly fact or fiction? Is it fair to my sisters that I hold these expectations of them? A reality check requires honest answers and necessary adjustments, which can save you and her some major grief.

Expectations of her that test too high (she needs to score 100 percent in every area of her being, and she never looks, acts, thinks, or makes you feel anything less than perfect) puts any woman at risk of eventual disqualification and dismissal ("You're okay but you're just not the one for me").

Black women have seen it and heard it all before. The let-them-down-easy dismissals, the men who romance them, then come up missing in action, or those who swore to them "You are definitely the one for me" only later to insist "You're not really who I thought you were, you deceived me." Each woman longs to be known for who they are and loved and accepted as they are. Although what they are can be quite impressive, they never will measure up to or continue to measure up to any man's unrealistic, perfectionistic fantasy image. That's too much to expect from love or any lover.

THE BOTTOM LINE

Men at work: Check in with reality. Simplify your expectations of your mate and of yourself. If you keep ending up discovering relationship after relationship, year after year, to have been "not quite what I was looking for," you need to readjust what you are looking for.

The benefits: When your expectations and tastes are based upon reasonable reality-based standards, you are inclusive rather than limited in your choice of mate.

The costs: That nagging suspicion that if you had just held out a little longer you "coulda/woulda" finally gotten your Ms. Right and life would have been right forever.

2. ▲ ■ ● ◆) Give Her Your Love in Her Language

To the man who loves me:
It's not at all a secret. If you pay close attention, I'm showing you all the time the ways I love to be loved. Please pay attention.

—From the Black woman you love

When it's all said and done, much of your success in loving a Black woman finally hinges on your willingness and ability to give her, when you can and as best you can, the kind of love she gives you. Though it's unrealistic for us to demand that we get it that way all the time, human beings love to be shown love that is an exact replica of the best aspects of the love we've shown others. In fact, our tendency is to measure expectations of another person's way of loving by comparing it to the standards set by our own ways. When you are sure that you deeply love someone, it's easy to conclude that the ways that you are naturally inclined to express your love (your "love language") are exactly how your mate will do it too if "she really loves you." Wrong.

Deep inside in the place where we draw conclusions about things, the thinking generally goes something like this: a) Since I am sure that what I feel for you is real love, and b) Since my love prompts me to think, feel, and perform in certain very positive ways toward you, then these ways of relating must be the way real loves works; therefore c) If you have real love for me, then your ways of relating to me should look exactly like the ways I relate to you. *No*

At least three things are true about the foregoing piece of logic. 1) It's what makes women expect that the men who love them (if the love is real) will naturally offer an abundant supply of self-disclosure, emotional expressiveness, collaborative spirit, and intimacy that is constantly shown and reaffirmed through words and feelings. 2) It's what makes men expect that the women who love them (if the love is real) will naturally offer an abundance of goal-oriented, dependable, no-nonsense emotional restraint, a high-performance approach to concrete, pragmatic issues, and trust and respect that is constantly expressed by allowing him freedom and independence. 3) It's what has kept men and women both "speaking" and "hearing" only one love language—their own!

How can the two of you who speak a love language foreign to the other ever be sure each other's love is real? You both must become bilingual of course! For you that will mean you keep on showing love in your native masculine style (to give it up is suicide and an unnecessary compromise) but that you also become a student of your woman's way of loving you in her language. And that you express your love for her in that language as well.

THE BOTTOM LINE

Men at work: Observe the ways your woman relates to you because she loves you. Take note of the kinds of things she likes to tell you, give you, and do for you and how she does those things. These make up her love language. Turn the tables. As often as possible make the deliberate choice to speak, give, and demonstrate your love for her in those ways.

The benefits: It's the closest you can come to hitting the bull's-eye in loving her. It's what most naturally, truly feels like real love to her (that's why she offers it to you) and it doesn't even require that she translate your love language. You'll already be speaking hers.

The costs: The possibility of some mechanical and awkward feelings as you do what *doesn't* come naturally, as well as all the time it may take to learn to do it.

3. ▲ ■ ● ◆ ◗
Expect to Have to Earn Her Trust

To the man who loves me:
It's very hard for me to let you know my feelings all the time
because I'm not always sure what you might do with them.
Actually, I wish I could have a signed guarantee that you'll
handle me right. I don't give my trust quickly or easily, but I
do want to place my trust in you. I just need to watch you
awhile.

—From the Black woman you love

No doubt you've already discovered that women pay very close attention to what is and is not happening in their relationships with their men. She silently, carefully observes you closely, charting the consistency of your words, your disposition, and your behavior toward her. She's constantly assessing both facts and feelings to determine how secure the foundation of your love is.

To your woman, love means giving more and more of herself to you. More physical, spiritual, and emotional access, more of her hopes, her vulnerability, and especially her trust. She won't give these treasures to you if she doesn't trust you. If you want her trust, you have to earn it.

Instinctively, she knows there is much at risk if she deposits too much of her vulnerable self too quickly. She knows she could end up hurt and taken advantage of. Love that doesn't offer her some security is not love at all to her.

It's nothing personal, not arrogant, conceited, requirements she imposes just to keep you busy while she decides what, if anything, she wants to do with you. Measuring your trustworthiness is the necessary and ongoing work she does when she sincerely wants to give herself fully to a loving relationship.

THE BOTTOM LINE

Men at work: You can earn her trust by your commitment to make few promises but by keeping the ones you make, by handling her with sensitivity and respect, and by being consistent, honest, and attracted to who she is now rather than who you'd like her to become. Refuse to show resentment about being so closely watched and evaluated for trustworthiness. Allow it, and behave toward her in ways that stand up to the test.

The benefits: Earning her trust by your consistency and integrity makes her feel secure and frees her to love you and receive love from you unreservedly. The higher her level of trust in you the lower the demand that you work to prove it. Freedom for you. She'll trust you until you give her good reason not to.

The costs: You may feel you are trying to swim upstream against a strong current. You'll discover that it's extremely difficult to undo the painful effects of a previous man's untrustworthiness. You'll have to determine if her trust can be gained, and if all the extra effort to get it is worth it.

4. Be Responsive to Her Without Taking Responsibility for Her

To the man who loves me:
I am incredibly blessed to have you in my life. I depend on
you being there for me when I'm up against something. My
life can be hard to handle sometimes. I count on you to handle
it with me though, not for me.

—From the Black woman you love

If you think that every burden, problem, need, want, struggle, fear, challenge, or flaw that your woman has is your responsibility to remove from her life, you are going to bite off far more than you can chew. When you take responsibility for the parts of a Black woman's life that only she and God are responsible for, you won't succeed and you'll end up exhausted.

Too often men have bought into the idea that "real manhood" means you must provide the woman you love a pain-free existence, totally unaffected by the harsh realities of her life. When the men who love Black women offer a love that merely buffers, shields, or takes possession of all her pains and problems, to keep her comfortable at all costs, then the love is counterfeit and ultimately an insult to her ability and a hell of a lot of pressure for you.

It can feed your cherished sense of significance and promise great potential earnings in applause when you set yourself up as her safety net. But don't be fooled. The process by which human beings grow wiser, more disciplined, fulfilled, and mature is struggle. Struggle hurts but it strengthens as well. She deserves every bit of the strength that comes from her struggle.

Be responsive (to) her rather than take responsibility (for) her. To be responsive means you care and you show it by your concern, your availability, and your support. Responsiveness and responsibility are different in their motives, their intent, and their strategy, even in their vocabulary:

- When she's worried and afraid, responsibility says, "Relax, sweetheart, I'll take over your life from here." Responsiveness says, "I see you're really upset, how can I help you in what you're dealing with?"
- When she's confused and indecisive, responsibility says, "Here, I'll figure it out for you. Just do what I tell you and you won't have to worry about this anymore." Responsiveness says, "I'm your sounding board. If you want to talk, I want to listen. And if you'd like, I'll give you my opinion."
- When she's in conflict with someone, responsibility says, "Let me handle this, I'm going to set them straight for you right now." Responsiveness says, "I know you must really be upset that you and ——— have fallen out. Do you want to talk about it?"
- When she's bored and apathetic, responsibility says, "I promise I will figure out a way to pull you out of the doldrums. Just give me a minute, I'll come up with something, you'll see." Responsiveness says, "It seems like you're itching to do something. I'm available if you decide you want us to do something together."

Everyone who ever learned to live richly, competently, and triumphantly learned to endure the aches and pains that go with taking responsibility for self. Don't rob the woman in your life of her productive struggles. Let her stand on her own two feet—even if her knees buckle from time to time. If you stand with her, in support, you will bless her. Standing for her will surely curse her.

THE BOTTOM LINE

Men at work: Look at your own life where you have seen necessary struggles and have taken responsibility for your life. Haven't you seen that it produces needed growth and maturity and ability for you? Are you helping or hindering that process in the Black woman you love? Make changes accordingly.

The benefits: By becoming responsive to her, instead of taking responsibility for her, you will be able to witness first-hand the leftover traces of "little girl" becoming "phenomenal woman" in the one you love.

The costs: If you stop taking responsibility for her life, you may suffer from a nagging guilt feeling and the self-deflating idea that she doesn't really need you. You could also suddenly be falsely accused by your woman of becoming uncaring, insensitive, and abandoning her in her struggles.

5. ▲▶ Don't Start What You Won't Continue

To the man who loves me:
I remember some of those sweet caring things you used to do
all the time just because you loved me. I wonder what it means
about your love for me that you don't do them anymore.

—From the Black woman you love

It may be a well-kept secret but the men who love Black women are more than able to perform the good deeds that demonstrate that love. You've certainly got what it takes to dream up and deliver the right stuff, and if the truth be known you have sometimes shown glimpses of greatness when you thought to do good works as simple as opening the door for her, calling her just to say hi, leaving her a tenderly worded love letter, greeting her with a warm embrace, or remembering her birthday. And you have performed some dramatic fancy gestures as well, like staying bedside with her through a sick spell, surprising her with tickets to visit her mother, or when you moved across the country because of *her* job transfer.

But a word of caution is in order here. Don't start delivering what you won't continue to. Because more important than having started doing a good thing is to continue it with consistency. Over the long haul, when it's no longer cute or clever or convenient to do so. But you keep it up anyway because it is a good work and because it expresses your love, and because you were at some point persuaded that she was well worth it. That kind of treatment, once begun, must continue. To stop (and you are still physically able to continue) sends the message that you no longer find her worth the work. Even if the Black woman you love has a powerful sense of self-worth, believing that her worth to you has diminished feels more painful and lonely than you might ever know. It would have been far less painful for her if you had never even started to offer those endearing good deeds than to have started them and stopped.

THE BOTTOM LINE

Men at work: Think through the little extras—those kind gestures you offer your woman—*before* you start doing them. Require of yourself an honest answer to the question: "Am I willing to keep doing this for her, forever?" If you know you're only willing for a "one-shot deal" and not a long-term one, you should a) Tell her how long she may expect it, or b) Avoid that gesture from the jump.

The benefits: Maintaining consistency in performing both the small- and the grand-scale acts that honor your mate makes your love visible and concrete to her. Your consistency, discipline, and responsiveness here add to the character and quality of your masculinity.

The costs: Like it or not, once you've started it, your behavior indicates an unspoken but binding commitment to continue it. Being bound to anything—even an unspoken relational contract like this—can be burdensome over time. But this kind of commitment can't be harmlessly withdrawn by merely announcing, "Sorry, I just don't feel like doing that anymore."

6. ▲ ■ Accept Her for Who She Is Now (Not Who You Think You Can Make Her Into)

To the man who loves me:
I get the impression that there really is no such thing as
being enough, in your eyes. Just when I start to believe you
are content with me as I am, you raise the requirements
again.

—From the Black woman you love

(Loving your woman's potential more than you love who she is now insults her.) Black women despise any attempt to shape, mold, or re-create them according to your idea of who and how they should be. Aside from the fact that you have no right to do it, she's most disturbed that how she already is—her looks, thoughts, and the many unique facets of her personality, how she lives her life and shows her love—doesn't rate high enough on your scale. In relationships, some of her deepest hurts revolve around the feeling that your love, devotion, and appreciation for her have to be paid for by camouflaging, or endlessly "refining" what makes her, her. It's like hearing the painful "You are just not enough for me as you are" repeated over and over again. No matter how high her self-esteem is, that's a message that can wilt her spirit; for many Black women it has made dealing with us too hurtful to want to attempt again.

Of course, none of this means you should feel guilty for having observed some things about her that could stand improvement or that you'd like to see changed to suit your personal tastes and preferences. For you to have an opinion is no crime. For you to take her as your mate, then subtly require her to fit your opinion before she can earn your best love, commitment, and affection *is* a crime. That's loving her potential and possibilities more than the person she is. You don't have to establish a relationship with her if the way she is is not acceptable to you, but if you take her, take her because you can love her sincerely and lavishly as she is today. Not because of who she might or might not become tomorrow.

She desires the kind of respect and acceptance that recognizes that change in another human being is something you may lovingly influence, but cannot produce. Not even with all the punishing, withholding, critiquing, coaching, threatening, and manipulating in the world. People change and improve when *they* hunger for it and work toward it, not when you or anyone else has that hunger for them. The Black woman in your life thrives on the assurance that though she's not finished growing, developing, and polishing who she is, she can rest in the assurance that you enthusiastically accept and embrace the woman she is right now.

THE BOTTOM LINE

Men at work: Ask and answer this crucial question: "Can I, will I love and share my best with this woman if in all our tomorrows she stays exactly the way she is today?" If the answer is no, decide what can *you* change in yourself, in order for you to be more fully committed to who she is now. Cease any efforts, both subtle and overt, to re-create her in any way or to penalize her for not becoming your ideal.

The benefits: One of the mysterious paradoxes of real life is that women are most willing to "become" when they feel accepted as they come.

The costs: Living with the possibility that she won't ever become exactly what you had hoped for, or that the process will take too long. You may be tempted to try heavy-handed tactics to "guarantee" she grows into your ideals. That will only make it worse.

7. ▲ ■ ● ◆) *Study Other Men*

To the man who loves me:
Many times I've seen in you some of the best qualities of my father, my brothers, and some of my closest men friends. I've wondered how this could be all wrapped up in one unique individual. It's a fascinating thing to me that you have taken the best qualities of others and made them your own.

—From the Black woman you love

Loving a woman the way she needs to be loved without compromising yourself requires huge amounts of wisdom, stamina, and experience. There is no step-by-step formula, college course, or genetic marker that can make anyone automatically skilled at it. Those who have achieved success got it by on-the-job training. No matter how much you have going for yourself and how well you're already doing at loving a Black woman, you could waste your most valuable resource if you don't study other men who love Black women well. Watch them closely and you'll learn valuable, practical lessons that can only enrich and encourage you as you strive to give and get the most satisfying love.

In everything in which you've achieved success, somebody else's good example, wise input, and generous encouragement helped you to make it so.

Don't be fooled into identifying men who love Black women well, based solely on how many women occupy their lives. As it relates to love, quantity and quality are two altogether different matters. "Quality men" are the ones who are not hung up on proving how much man they are. Not to their women, not to other men, and not to themselves. Quality men have no problem being seen serving their women with humility or protecting them with ferocity or committing to their integrity. They don't just like women for what they can get from them. Rather, they are fascinated by them and truly love them. They have learned how to relate to them in ways that honor women and make them feel adored, cherished, and secure. Take note of them. Listen and follow their example. The quality of your own skill and sensitivity will be enhanced.

Get back some of your time that is too often spent listening to the advice of men who are only bragging, lying, or female bashing. The proof is in the pudding. Where you see no woman in their life or where you see a frustrated, unhappy one, that man should be no mentor for you. Instead, look around for the man who's standing beside a Black woman who is positively glowing with that air of joy and satisfaction, and the man whose face lights up when the woman he loves enters the room. And the one who offers himself and his treasures to her generously, with no hint of shame or selfishness.

If you know one like him, study him. Don't get hung up on how old or young or plain or fancy he may be. Learn from him. If you are one yourself, look around. Some man, or several, could be watching you. Teach them right. Black women everywhere will be extremely grateful.

THE BOTTOM LINE

Men at work: Dare to talk seriously with other men about women and love. Approach the subject with the same kind of interest you show your career, sports, politics, or money. Enlist a qualified "relationship mentor"—an older, experienced "woman-friendly" brother with whom you commit to share the details of your romantic life, and from whom you are willing to accept wise counsel. Be open and honest when you share with him. Then dare to really listen and apply the best of your mentor's advice.

The benefits: The primary benefit is that like in every other area of endeavor your own game will get better when you have the model of a "master" to observe. The secondary benefit is that the woman you love will reap the rewards of the heightened levels of skill and sensitivity you'll get by refusing to be limited to just what you know about loving a Black woman. Other men's relationship success stories can help you become even more of a success story yourself.

The costs: The time and humility it takes to study other men is like the time it takes to study a textbook. To say nothing of the fact that attempting to learn from others makes some men feel as if they're admitting that their own skill level is inferior.

8. ▲ ● ◗ Don't Require That Your Every Move Be Applauded

To the man who loves me:
Maybe it's not fair, but I wish appreciation and respect for
you and the good things you do could be enough. I get the
impression that you really want me to make a big deal out
of every single good thing you do. Could that be true? Every
single thing?

—From the Black woman you love

Whatever you may try to accomplish in any area of your life, you are likely to keep working at it more enthusiastically and ultimately more successfully if you get some acknowledgment, recognition, and applause along the way. It's just as true as you work to follow the advice in this book and show the Black woman in your life the kind of love she most needs. When she notices and commends your efforts, it makes keeping up the good work much easier and more appealing because it's got some personal reward for you.

The real challenge, though, is continuing to do what's right because it's right—even if your woman, or everyone else, fails to applaud you for doing it. When you require that your every positive act be given a standing ovation, or at least some honorable mention, you'll become dependent on her actions to motivate yours. You've got far too much self-sufficiency, tenacity, and initiative inside you to need ego strokes in order to perform. *Want* them? Always. *Need* them? Never!

In a perfect world the woman you love would always be the first one to look you in your eyes and declare with sincerity, "You did that so well" or "I appreciate the respectful way you treat me" or "You keep proving over and over to me that you are an incredible man." In the real world she'll sometimes be too distracted, self-involved, or just plain too tired to applaud you. In fact, she may have more to say about the few things you did poorly than the many things you did well. But when you're motivated from within you, your excellence carries its own rewards.

Get used to applauding and affirming yourself. If you are a good man you didn't become one just because a woman was thrilled by your being one.

THE BOTTOM LINE

Men at work: Let her applause become a fringe benefit, not the fuel you need to live your life, and show your love to the best of your ability according to the highest possible standards. Continue under your own steam if need be.

The benefits: Though the Black woman in your life may love to applaud you and your positive efforts, if she believes you can't or won't function without it, she'll get sick of that real fast. When you are perfectly willing and able to do it for yourself, your woman respects and admires your self-motivated strength—which will be highly esteemed in her eyes and, in one way or another, thunderously applauded by her.

The costs: You may suffer some lonely, underappreciated, and resentful feelings if you have to withdraw, cold turkey, from your addiction to applause.

9. ▲ Tell Her Exactly What Your Commitment Means

To the man who loves me:
I've known you long enough to see. You're a man who doesn't
waste words. I usually don't have to guess where you stand.
Except when it comes to where you stand about us. I'm really
getting confused because I hear you say a lot of words, but
I'm still not sure exactly what you are offering me.

—From the Black woman you love

Ask a thousand Black women what is the most important desire they have of the men in their lives and you're likely to hear repeated a thousand times the word "commitment." Your woman, or the one on her way, wants to know what the two of you are to each other and what that does or does not mean about your future together. She knows she can only speak for herself and her perceptions and desires, and that she can in no way define or demand what your commitment level must be. But you can be sure she's determined to know the truth about the matter and she can only get that from you.

In every phase of your relationship with her, it will be crucial that you clarify what your commitment level is and is not. As much as you may resist the idea of being pinned down to a specific answer, which of course closes off some of the options that being vague allows you, she needs to know.

If she doesn't know she's left to assume. And if she assumes, she's likely to be wrong—over- or underestimating—the seriousness of your commitment to her. If she's wrong, her expectations of you and her efforts in the relationship will be out of sync with the truth. That's a surefire setup for tragic misunderstandings, bitter conflicts, and yet another severed relationship. But even bigger than that, there's then more mistrust, more hostility, and more alienation between Black women and their men. Enough already.

Be thorough and above all be honest. If your present commitment level is such that you're going out with her, and others too, say so. If you're going for broke, offering a serious and exclusive relationship, declare it. If it's only a close friendship and running-partner commitment that you have in mind, come clean and tell her that. If your feelings for her run deep, but marriage is definitely not on your mind, again, say so. Then say and do only that which is consistent with your stated level of commitment and nothing else. Don't confuse things by declaring one commitment level and relating to her in a manner that is only appropriate to another. She will feel deceived and taken advantage of. Mismatched or unclear commitment between you and the woman in your life is among the most potentially hazardous areas of a relationship. Best not to play charades with her emotions, waiting until she demands that you make your intentions known. With little to no commitment clarity from you, women are liable to press you for an answer far too early in the game—or way too late.

THE BOTTOM LINE

Men at work: In spite of the fears of disappointing or losing her, tell her the truth, the whole truth, and nothing but the truth about what you're offering her, then govern yourself accordingly. The depth of your expressions of intimacy and degree of exclusivity should match the level of commitment you have made to her and the relationship.

The benefits: Maximum clarity means minimal confusion. There is so much more potential for a loving, mutually satisfying relationship when you are both on the same page about your level of commitment to each other. It will keep your woman from giving over too much to you or holding back from you when she is unsure about where you stand.

The costs: Having to think through your commitment level and be pinned down to a precise declaration and demonstration of it. Also, the possibility that what you are offering is something more or less or different from what she has in mind for you. That way, one of you could end up with hurt feelings.

10. ◆ ⟩ *Listen to Her Problems Without Rushing to Solve Them*

To the man who loves me:
No matter how frustrated I may sound when I share my troubles with you, don't be fooled into thinking I'm asking you to make them all go away. I just want you to feel what I'm feeling and understand what I'm going through. I want to know that it is somehow as important to you as it is to me. It's the emotional equivalent of holding my hand.

—From the Black woman you love

When the woman you love flings open the door and invites you into the place where she deals with her problems, questions, and frustrations, you may be surprised to know that she isn't requiring or even requesting that you solve them all. Unless she thinks you are the problem—and she'll certainly let you know that—she's sharing her private struggles and concerns with you because talking it out with someone who cares for her is what women do. It's a crucial step in her way of solving her own problems.

Men's goal-oriented performance momentum is directed toward conquering the problems, not feeling them. Women first need to experience their problems on an emotional level, in effect "trying them on," in order to know how weighty and cumbersome they are. Women tend to feel their problems before they fix them. Talking helps them do that vital feeling work. Your role in all of this is to be her listening ear, allowing her to get at her feelings through her words.

Let her talk. Better yet, encourage her to. As you do, stifle your advice-giving, problem-solving tendency and listen to her with your whole mind and body focused on hearing her out, not rushing to help her out. Offer advice only upon request. Just listen as she talks in circles and stay strapped in next to her on the emotional roller-coaster ride.

Your woman is probably quite able to come up with solutions on her own (remember she had to before you came along), what she can't get alone is the powerfully affirming gift of your nonjudgmental attitude and your listening ears. Work to become her sounding board, not just her advice-dispensing life-management consultant.

THE BOTTOM LINE

Men at work: Practice active listening. Use attentive body language, clarifying questions, facial expressions, and other "I'm listening" signals that make it clear to her that serving her is more important to you than the significance boost you get from solving her problems.

The benefits: You get to put away your hard hat and fix-it equipment and relax. You are free to ignore your compulsion to repair her problems for her. She gets to have your intimate companionship as she processes her situation, in her own way.

The costs: It may be extremely difficult when she needs you to listen to her about problem feelings that have to do with you. You may be tempted to explain or defend yourself or correct what seem to you inaccurate or emotionally overwrought criticisms. Though it may not at first seem so, you'll actually get to the resolution of these matters quicker, more cleanly, and more effectively if you allow her to talk it all out first.

11. ■● *Refer to All Black Women with Respect*

To the man who loves me:
I wonder if you even notice it anymore, but there's some really foul stuff that comes out of your mouth when you're talking about women. It offends me. I've always shrugged it off because you never talk about me that way. Finally I realized what I don't think you have: I'm one of them that you're talking about. I'm a woman too.

—From the Black woman you love

Black women are always listening. The one you love is definitely paying attention to your choice of words, the labels you use, and the jokes you tell. She's measuring how much respect you have for her as a woman by how much you show for all women. She knows intuitively that if you are content to use words like "bitches," "broads," "hoes," and all their derogatory synonyms to refer to any female, then you're likely to use them or at least think them in reference to her as well. Above all she knows that if you'll refer to women in a nasty, low-down way, you're liable to treat them low-down and nasty too.

The clearest indications of how little a man values a woman is by how willing he is to:

- Make frequent demeaning and stereotypical references to women and Black women in particular.
- Use vulgarities to describe women that keys in on their physical or sexual attributes and ignores or denigrates their mental, emotional, and spiritual ones.
- Use or allow language that is mostly based on a repertoire of jokes, stories, and sayings at the expense of Black women.
- Settle arguments with her by launching a barrage of cruel put-downs and verbal jabs that he applies uniquely to women but never to men.

Words have awesome power to heal, to elevate, and to affirm. They also have the power to debase, violate, or to shape horribly destructive images. Once spoken they can't ever truly be taken back. What comes out of your mouth reveals the degree of respect and appreciation for your woman that's inside your heart.

Though she may laugh it off, ignore it, or refer to women herself in those vile terms, if you're serious about loving a Black woman according to what they most need and desire most from men, it's important that you develop and employ a vocabulary that refers to women with honor and the utmost respect.

Every verbal reference you make to your woman or any woman will either contribute to more negative, demeaning treatment of Black women or help do away with it.

THE BOTTOM LINE

Men at work: Evaluate your vocabulary, your attitude, and especially the labels and humor you use in reference to Black women. Do away with anything you wouldn't want anybody to use in reference to your mother.

The benefits: Black women have suffered terribly from the damaging and harmful images perpetuated about them through verbal disrespect. When you use only affirming and elevating speech, you send a message to her that she is valued and treasured and worthy of your demonstrated respect and that you can be trusted to give it.

The costs: The discipline and effort it takes to change whatever bad habits you may have developed in this area.

12. Take the Blame (But Only When It's Yours)

To the man who loves me:
What do you think will happen if you take the blame? When it's mine, I'll take it. When it's yours, I just want you to own up to it. It's a bold man who'll do that on his own.

—From the Black woman you love

One of life's biggest time-wasters and frustration-makers is the endless back and forth between you and the Black woman you love over who's to blame for that thing that happened that both of you wish hadn't happened. Whatever it was—an ill-informed accusation, a broken promise, an insensitive response, a bad attitude, or a bounced check—it's out there now for both of you to regret. Since it *did* happen and nothing can change that fact, you'd both prefer to be the victim rather than the perpetrator. Accepting blame can be a terrible assault on your pride, because it means you were wrong. Nobody likes to be wrong.

But when it's *your* imperfection that has shown through and caused some fallout between the two of you, the best thing you can do is take the blame. Own it, repent it, and get over it. Whether it's a little annoyance or a huge disaster, before you get around to any cleanup efforts or to looking for someone else's doorstep at which to lay it—take the blame.

Your strength of character and your boldness to look truth in the eye without being intimidated by it are highly appealing attributes to the woman in your life. When you take the blame that's rightfully yours, without copping a plea, glossing it over, or dancing around it, she sees the power of integrity. It's the kind of power that signals greatness. Women appreciate your goodness, but they absolutely marvel at your greatness, and the privilege of being intimately linked with the man who possesses it. I caution you, however, not to take blame that's not yours to take. When, out of frustration, resignation, guilt, or a desire to placate, silence, or patronize her, you claim guilt where you're really innocent, you are keeping the peace, but by forfeiting the truth. You can't afford to do that.

There is no nobility in taking the blame for what was not within your control or due to your actions. Nothing about being the man who loves her requires you to shift blame that

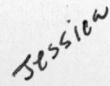

should be on her plate to yours. Start that habit and you'll be digging a deep hole that will swallow you both. Though she may allow you to do it and bask in the vindicating warmth, she'll figure out what you are up to—a quick, hassle-free way to become her hero. Eventually that will erode her respect for you—*and* for your sincerity. Which can do some serious damage to your self-respect as well.

THE BOTTOM LINE

Men at work: When you did it, plainly admit it: "It was my fault, I screwed up . . . I will correct the matter by . . ." (Note: Taking the blame means accepting responsibility, but not punishment, condemnation, or ridicule from her or from yourself.)

The benefits: When you take the blame that's yours and none that isn't, you short-circuit the possibility that she will ever put you up on a pedestal as a perfect, failure-free specimen. If you don't, you'll never be able to afford for your failures to be seen, or you'll come crashing down from that lofty pedestal.

The costs: Claiming responsibility for your wrong can stir up moderate to intense feelings of guilt and failure—what men most hate to feel.

13. ◆ *Never Compare Her*

To the man who loves me:
Have you noticed how often you mention that I'm a lot like
somebody else you know when you are paying me a compli-
ment or when getting on my case about something? Believe me,
I've noticed.

—From the Black woman you love

The woman you love or one day will love wants to experience the joy of knowing that your devotion, admiration, and affection is based on the unique person she is and the her and her alone mix of appealing attributes and fascinating qualities she possesses. Your woman doesn't want to even think that she stands in anyone else's shadow or that she is desirable to you because she somehow reminds you of somebody else. Even if she does, you need to keep that bit of information to yourself. Resist comparing her to any woman you've ever known at any time.

Though you may mean it as the ultimate compliment when you point out to the Black woman in your life that she is "just like . . ." or "on the same order as . . ." or "could be twins with . . ." any other female living or dead, famous or infamous, from your mother to Mother Teresa—she is not likely to be impressed. Rather, what she longs to hear from you are the wonderful things you've discovered in her that you have not discovered in anyone else. She yearns to know that she has, simply by being herself, filled a unique role and has a unique function in your life. She wants to know that to you, she is in a class all by herself, not one that's full to overflowing with images of every woman you have ever known.

Comparisons are so handy because they add color and clarity to your conversation, allowing you to make your point concisely and vividly: "My previous girlfriend/wife/lover didn't do it/say it/see it like that . . ." or "You look just like . . ." or (the worst of them) "I wish you were more like . . ." But loving her with skill and sensitivity requires that you work harder to make your point another way.

Black women already find themselves bedeviled by the tendency to compare themselves to too many narrow and preconceived images of feminine beauty, temperament, and conduct—from the super-models of the fashion magazines to the "nasty girls" of music videos to the heroines of fiction and film to the demure, homespun kind of women your grandmother described in detail, telling you not to stop till you get one like her.

Comparisons make it seem as though she's only as good as Ms. So-and-So or as no good as Ms. Such-and-Such. She treasures her individuality, and if you're not careful she's likely to hear your comparisons as a demand for her to be more like Ms. What's-Her-Name or less like Ms. Whatchamacallit. Black women place a high value on the freedom to be like themselves and nobody else.

Your woman relishes the assurance that on her own terms she is marvelously acceptable to you.

THE BOTTOM LINE

Men at work: Make a mental note to red-flag yourself whenever you use the phrase "just like" in reference to your mate. Back up and make your point to her some other way, comparison-free.

The benefits: The Black woman you *love* will benefit hugely from the assurance that she holds a singular place of honor and esteem in your eyes and not because she's better, worse, or just like anyone else.

The costs: Next to none. Other than losing out on the usefulness of comparisons when you want to communicate something positive about her. Lose the comparisons anyway.

14. ▲ ■ ● ◆ ◗ *Show Her Off*

To the man who loves me:
What really matters to me is not that other people are impressed with me, but that you are. Funny thing is though, when you parade me around and brag all over the place about me, that's how I find out how impressed you are with me.

—From the Black woman you love

A surefire way to make the Black woman you love feel absolutely adored and incredibly secure in your delight in her is to go out of your way to show her off. When your public behavior demonstrates just how proud you are to have her on your arm and in your life, you freshly reaffirm the high value you place on her. Your high estimation of her, how stunning she looks, how brilliant her mind is, how poised, charming, tenacious, talented, and unique she is, means more to her than anyone else's. Women thrive on knowing beyond a shadow of a doubt that you find their inner and outer assets captivating. You confirm it when you enthusiastically present to the "watching world" the woman who makes you proud.

It's boasting to others pure and simple that I'm talking

about. It's your unapologetic habit of bragging about your woman, whose attributes are worthy of your pointing out, declaring aloud, and making a fuss over—and you don't care who knows it. It's pure gold to her and her self-image and confidence in your love for her.

Showing her off is not for the sake of educating others about who you have and what she has going for herself. It's more about taking advantage of the opportunity you have to esteem her as you remind her that she is the woman who, with all her virtues, has stood out among women, and that you are honored that she stands beside you and shares her life with you.

THE BOTTOM LINE

Men at work: Take advantage of every possible opportunity you have to boast publicly about the things that most impress you about your mate. From time to time, go with her, sit in the back and support her in the settings where she performs impressively in her world of activities. Take care to introduce her to others with positive remarks.

The benefits: When you show her off, you dramatically enhance her self-image and her appreciation for your expressive, adoring kind of love. You will do much to ease the aches of self-doubt, any tendency she may have to struggle with feelings of unworthiness.

The costs: Expending the effort to discover and focus on the qualities you want to show off about her when they seem overshadowed by things you don't like about her. The repetition and the pressure to keep coming up with more. And the possibility that her self-image is so poor she'll be uncomfortable with you bragging about her.

15. ■ ● ◆ *Give Her the Space to Disappoint You*

To the man who loves me:
I can live with the fact that we'll let each other down some-
times. The best I have to offer you is imperfection—but with
my effort toward achieving perfection. I need this to be a
place where letting someone down is not life-threatening.

—From the Black woman you love

Make no mistake, in some ways, great and small, she will definitely blow it and you will hate it. She'll fail to do something she said she'd do (or she'll fail to do it right). She'll forget, ignore, misunderstand, lose it, leave it, or loan it out, and as far as you are concerned it will screw things up big-time. In spite of how much her imperfect performance ticks you off, an advanced-level skill in loving a Black woman is to give her the space to fail and to disappoint you without having to endure your criticism or punishment.

I'm not asking you to pretend you downright enjoyed her mess-up, and you'd love for her to do it all over again. But I am challenging you to pump up your patience and give some grace to the one you say you love. More than likely she'll be tremendously blessed to receive just the degree of patience and grace that you freely give yourself and the friends, co-workers, clients, and virtual strangers who daily mess up a little piece of your world. How is it that they so often get a gracious "That's okay, no big thing . . ." from you, and your woman too often gets a contempt-filled *"What in the world were you thinking about?"*

Grace is love on the highest order, because it's love granted to someone which isn't based on their performance. It's love they can count on from you, even when they admittedly haven't earned it.

Grace:
- Doesn't blindly ignore the failures of others, it just refuses to condemn them for it.
- Doesn't always keep meticulous mental records of the quality and quantity of a lover's every failure.
- Doesn't use "word-whippings" or nonverbal vengeance techniques to scold or demean.
- Doesn't penalize a partner by emotional or physical withdrawal.
- Doesn't lie, sending the message that the mess-up didn't matter, only to later quietly punish the offender as if it really did matter.
- Doesn't pretend your mate's failures are so uniquely different from your own.

Letting you down is one of a woman's greatest personal letdowns. They fervently seek after a harmonious and intimate bond of acceptance and affection with you. Unfortunately, your harsh rebukes or stinging silences can make her feel as if that all-important bond is severed.

THE BOTTOM LINE

Men at work: When she fails and disappoints you, commit to offering her no less than the kind of compassionate response you give yourself or to others who mean far less to you than she does. Watch your mouth, and your mood, in the aftermath of her mistakes.

The benefits: To grant her this kind of patience, under-standing, and sensitivity when she blows it will show you to be a man of tremendous compassion. To show grace and compassion to her requires an amazing amount of inner strength and self-assurance. Your compassion for her ignites her passion for you. Also, the more grace you give, the more you're likely to receive when *you* screw up.

The costs: To show grace and restraint will cost you that gratifying feeling of getting to play the role of outraged victim. Often men secretly treasure that feeling because it supports an "I'm right, you're wrong" attitude, which makes ego-boosting activities like indicting, instructing, and punishing her feel completely justified.

16. ▲ ■ ● ◆ ◗
Invest in the Things That Nourish Her

To the man who loves me:
Honestly, there's something I need to know. Do I mean
enough to you that you'll support the things in my life that
give me joy?

—From the Black woman you love

The greater part of building a wonderful relationship has to do with the two of you constantly making every kind of meaningful investment in each other's lives. Love is at its best when it's not all about "I'll get mine, you get yours." Instead it's the conscious, deliberate, and consistent search for ways that your efforts and contributions can enrich the life of the woman you love—and she's busy trying to do the same thing for you. Real love is evidenced by the quantity and quality of things you support in your woman's life and provide for her life to nourish her mind, body, and soul.

Nourishing your woman's life is not a vague abstract concept. It is as practical and specific as the things one must do to nourish any living thing to cause it to thrive and flourish, not merely exist. Feeding, watering, securing, examining, and making provisions for it cause everything in creation to grow, including the Black woman you love.

You nourish her:

- When you invest in the things that enrich her life.
- When you encourage and support her efforts to advance her education, career, or her physical, spiritual, or mental well-being.
- When you accept and make accommodations for the time she needs for adequate solitude, reflection, or revitalization even though it may temporarily take her away from you.
- When you offer her some of the things she doesn't absolutely need but that bring her tremendous joy, like flowers, massages, "the works" at the beauty salon, or a hot bath you've readied for her.
- When you take her most cherished aspirations seriously and rally your own resources to help her achieve them.
- When you insist she go "off duty" and "waste" some time and money on herself.

When you nourish her life in these ways it shows that you place a high value on something simply because the woman you love does. It says to her, "I treasure the things that are special to you because they are special to you." What you are really saying is, "I treasure you."

THE BOTTOM LINE

Men at work: Stay alert to discover what things put a spark of delight in your woman's eyes. Then do everything in your power to provide its consistent presence in her life. Feel free to ask her what's on the list of the most treasured and soul-nourishing things in her private world and how you can help make them happen; listen, then act immediately.

The benefits: She will feel positively adored by you. She'll flourish in the assurance that you care enough about what she cares about to invest in the things that switch on her "pleased, satisfied, and content" button. It's also a beneficial way for you to uphold the value of her paying attention to enriching her own life, rather than only how she can enrich everybody else's.

The costs: Investing heavily in the things that nourish her provides no guarantee that you'll get as much as you give. If you see this as a "contract" rather than a "contribution" with no strings attached, you could easily fall into the trap of trying to keep score of whose turn it is to nourish whom.

17. ■● *Lighten Up*

To the man who loves me:
You look so responsible, determined, and cool, very cool, all
the time. I have sometimes wondered why you have such a
stern, serious personality. I don't know why, but I think there
might also be a laughing, fun-loving boy inside you. At least
I hope there is because I really want to know him.

—From the Black woman you love

If you are the kind of man who always takes care of business, and is a plan-maker and problem-solver, who believes that loving her right is serious business with no room for clowning, you are likely to have impressed the woman you love, yourself, and everybody else. Deep thinkers with their serious-minded approach to life and love are looked up to by everybody. But you are also likely to have driven yourself, your woman, and everybody else crazy with your stiff no-nonsense personality. You might be surprised to know that the Black woman you love hopes that one day you'll relax, lighten up, and laugh a little.

Serious soldiers like you are determined not to be found guilty of finger-popping and good-timing their way through life. They are always stiffly at attention because to stand at ease for even a moment will look foolish and because they fear that something might fall apart if they do. They believe a sense of humor is all right for some brothers, but even better is a cool, unflappable, and thoroughly controlled demeanor. To look and act in the other way could be perceived as being goofy and, worse yet, weak.

But when your actions and especially your attitude display an "all work and no play" mind-set, you have erased out, or safely locked away, one huge part of who you are—your humor. Your sense of humor is your God-given ability to engage responsibly in life and laugh at it, and yourself, at the same time.

As much as your woman may respect your sober-mindedness she would probably love to fall out on the floor and laugh with you, or even at you. Your relationship is not about being "on it" and keeping everything in check twenty-four hours a day. Often it is silly fun and games, and for the two of you to share in that part together adds another dimension to the intimacy of your relationship. You needn't compete with Eddie Murphy, Martin Lawrence, or Bill Cosby. It's not your job to make her laugh. But it is your chance to let the Black woman you love have access to the part of you where pure, spontaneous, unmonitored humor takes over and where you get to smile, laugh hysterically, or even lose it. That'll only happen if, for a moment, you drop your heavy load, lighten up, and let her in.

THE BOTTOM LINE

Men at work: Challenge yourself to lighten your demeanor and laugh more. Simply refuse to hold in, cover up, or flee from your humor or laughter. While you're at it, cease your subtle efforts to silence her humor. Make time for fun with her that doesn't accomplish anything on your to-do list or run the risk of making you feel or look foolish.

The benefits: If you work on lightening up, both of you will gain a new freedom in your relationship with fewer inhibitions and more genuine fun. You'll have another part of you for her to connect with, to appreciate, and to admire.

The costs: The awkwardness and risk of letting down your cool, humorless persona. Your insides insist that doing so will make you vulnerable to criticism and ridicule and the embarrassment they bring.

18. ▲ *Get Serious*

To the man who loves me:
When there is something kind of crazy and laughable going on in my life I usually can't wait to share that with you. With your sense of humor I always know you're going to say something that will make me die laughing. I wish it weren't so, but when it's something kind of serious going on, something that can't be played with, it usually doesn't even occur to me to share that with you.

—From the Black woman you love

The Black woman in your life is counting on you for so much. Your approach to life and every element of it has a great deal of meaning to her. It's what she measures to determine how much strength and character you have stored up on the inside and how wise or unwise it is for her to open her life to you. Though she may admire, and even envy, your footloose, fun-loving style, if that's all you've got, she'll only see you as a nice playmate, not a mature partner she can count on. You'll make her laugh, and she'll have a ball, but when it comes down to the weightier matters of life she'll want you to get serious and get going.

There's absolutely nothing wrong with you not trying to

rule the world or not approaching everything as if it were a life-or-death matter. Your outrageous sense of humor and your delight in the simple pleasures of life are very attractive qualities that catch her eye and win her heart. But if they are not balanced by your willingness to get serious, make tough decisions, and handle the hard stuff that makes life and love work, then giving you the respect that's due a strong, responsible man will be difficult for her. She'll have, at best, the fleeting affection she'd give to a clown at the circus or an old teddy bear on her shelf.

You can stand to add to your serious side if:

- Your spending on toys, gadgets, and good times keeps you behind on your financial obligations or from ever building up any wealth.
- You can't help trying to turn heavy conversations with your woman into jokes that take you off the subject.
- At the end of the day you have efficiently accomplished the tasks you do enjoy and few if any of those you don't.
- You nonchalantly avoid definitive decision-making, constantly declaring "I'm going to . . ." and seldom getting around to it.
- You sail from one relationship to another when your mate's expectations and emotions start getting serious.

THE BOTTOM LINE

Men at work: Identify the few or many ways you use humor and fun to avoid, delay, or deny the serious side of your life and your relationships. Don't wait until it feels right; make serious changes now that will bring balance.

The benefits: Her respect and your self-respect will increase because you prove to yourself that you're a man of substance and seriousness who balances your appealing humor and calm demeanor. She can count on you and admire and enjoy both sides of your personality.

The costs: Decision-making. Confrontation of hard issues and speaking seriously from the depths of your heart, not just your humor, are necessary and beneficial but they are seldom fun.

19. ▲ ■ ◆ *Say "I Don't Know" When You Don't*

To the man who loves me:
One of the first things that attracted me to you was your
intelligence. You are a very wise man. But I'm smart enough
to know that you couldn't possibly know everything about
everything. I hate it when a man tries to act as if he does.

—From the Black woman you love

From time to time the Black woman in your life will ask questions. Probably lots of them. They may be simple yes-or-no ones, probing "how do you really feel about this" ones, or deep intellectual "what's your point of view" ones, and perhaps most frequently, advice-seeking "what do you think I ought to do about . . ." ones. Whatever she may ask, when you have an honest answer, give it—when you don't, admit it: "I don't know."

They may seem like the three hardest-to-say words in the English language. Even though the phrase may feel like a two-ton boulder wedged in your throat—open your mouth and let it out!

Let's face it, there really is something in men that tempts us to believe that if women could come up with the questions we should know the answers—and we think they think we should know it too. We'd actually prefer that our women didn't ask, in the first place, questions that we don't have ready answers to. It really can throw us off when they do. That's why you've probably heard this little scenario, or something like it, over and over:

She says: "Baby, I was wondering, do you think I should_____or not, because you know_____, and I have to___, so that_____."

He says: (here is where "I don't know" should have been inserted. Instead she hears): "Why are you asking me? I don't see why you can't figure some things out by yourself!"

She says (hurt and offended): "All I did was ask you a simple question. You could have just said yes or no!"

"I don't know" can be a very honest and perfectly legitimate response. The truth that can set you free is that you don't have to have all the answers—you don't even have to find out all the answers—and contrary to how you may feel, she's probably not requiring that you do, either.

Fact is, often women are actually trying to demonstrate respect for their men by seeking and valuing your opinions and input. It's yet another way that they try to point out your power and ability—for your sake and for their own, because they feel even more secure when reminded that they are linked up to someone powerful.

Aside from information-seeking, women love to ask questions of the men in their lives because it reinforces for them the idea that we are working on life together—collaboration. Your input is another reassurance that her "us thing" with you is solid and secure.

So when you get a sulky attitude, promise to get an answer, then don't, or just plain ignore her, you break a very meaningful link between the two of you and chip away at one of her key security and intimacy bricks.

For the record, "I don't know" should never be used as an "escape clause," or a handy verbal device to keep from doing some emotional or mental work that you don't feel like doing. If what she's inquiring about is something about you that she can only find out from you and it really is something important for the woman you love to have access to, "I don't know" won't do. Promise her an honest answer, then deliver one.

THE BOTTOM LINE

Men at work: The next time "I don't know" is your honest response to her question, add a "but..." statement to it that suggests that although you have no insights, opinions, or advice at the moment, the Black woman you love and her issue matter to you. For example: "I don't know, but that *is* an important question..." or "I don't know, but please let me know what you end up deciding about that" or "I don't know, but ask me again tomorrow."

The benefits: She'll admire and deeply appreciate your humility, your honesty, and your concern—she's not likely to forget any of them very easily or quickly. Then she'll move on to get the answers she needs. Additionally, admitting you don't know, when you don't, will relieve you of the self-imposed pressure of "needing" to be the All-Wise, All-Seeing, All-Knowing One, freeing you to just be a good man who knows some of the answers but not all of them.

The costs: When men are sure they have the answers, they feel "more man." When, for whatever the reason, you don't have them, you may feel a little or a lot "less man."

20. ▲ ■ ● ◆ ❯ Tell Her What You Assume She Already Knows

To the man who loves me:
Yes, I am quite intuitive, and yes, I can figure out some
things very well without any explanations. I may know a lot,
but when it comes to you and us, I don't want to just think I
know, I want to be sure I do.

—From the Black woman you love

Don't assume she knows anything about your love for her unless you tell her. Though it may seem to you that your actions have made it loud and clear and that she has somehow figured out your feelings for her by silent observation, she needs the words. She needs you to plainly and repeatedly tell her what you think she should already know. For the Black woman in your life, your skillful use of nouns, verbs, and adjectives, sentences, and paragraphs ensures her more clarity and accuracy in knowing exactly where she stands in your desire, your devotion, and your commitment. Your non-verbal cues—what you do and what you don't ever do—say and are very significant indications of your love. But to your woman, the spoken word wins hands down, every time, because she can at best only make assumptions as to the meaning behind your actions or behaviors. She can't be totally sure of things unless you speak up and spell it out:

- Don't assume that she knows you are thoroughly impressed with her talents and abilities, tell her.
- Don't assume that she already knows you admire her courage and determination, tell her.
- Don't assume that she already knows you love her deeply and you'd hate to do without her, tell her.
- Don't assume that she already knows you are not ready for an exclusive relationship and are still seeing other women, tell her.

For women, an intimate and secure relationship with balance, harmony, and mutual appreciation is the goal. She can be sure of how *she* feels about you, but confirming how *you* feel about *her* is best done with words—your words. When you verbalize those feelings, you erase some of the doubts and insecurities that can plague her in her relationship with you. Work to boost the security of the woman you love. She may not be as self-assured as she appears. She can be especially helped by your taking the time to communicate your reassuring facts and feelings about your pride in her and about how much you care for her.

Your Black woman can give and be and do so much in the name of love when she knows what you know about her. Though she may never ask, she yearns to know with assurance.

THE BOTTOM LINE

Men at work: What are some of the most important facts about your feelings for and commitment to your woman that you hope she knows but you haven't clearly articulated to her? Put them into words. Explain until she gets it just the way you feel it and mean it.

The benefits: To a great extent women are prone to measure much of themselves by the degree to which they have benefited someone else's life. For them being a successful woman has a lot to do with nurturing others. It is not uncommon for them to feel as if they give so much of it, and get so little back. When you clearly make known how much her love means to you, and the depth of your commitment to her, the scales begin to balance. Balance is overwhelmingly satisfying to her.

The costs: The challenge of putting your hard-to-express feelings into words. Trying to find concrete words instead of leaving her to rely upon unverified assumptions and vague unconfirmed thoughts.

21. ▲ ■ ● ◆ ▶ *Read Between the Lines*

To the man who loves me:
Yes, I do mean what I say, and, no, I don't expect you to
have to play a guessing game. But I do need you to know
that when I speak to you, everything about what I say and
how I say it has some meaning. Please don't just focus on
my words alone and miss my message.

—From the Black woman you love

Advanced-level skills in loving a Black woman involve:

1. Carefully listening to everything she says to you.
2. Reading between the lines to get her fullest meaning.
3. Confirming with her what you think you heard.

To increase the love and intimacy level between you as well as to keep the lines of communication flowing freely, you'll do well to practice this tricky three-step process until you're a master at it.

When she is satisfied that your love is both plentiful and available, she'll begin to share more and more of herself with you. She'll have a strong urge to communicate her ideas, her feelings, and her desires to the man who loves her. As she does, and as your response makes it clear that you are truly interested, her love builds some more . . . and she'll reveal some more . . . and the cycle will repeat itself. For your woman this is intimacy at its most fulfilling.

The tricky part is knowing that the deeper the bond of closeness grows between you, the more her sharing is likely to flow forth naturally, spontaneously, and often without the benefit of the helpful whys and wherefores, the background information that clarifies what she means. And though her message may have more depth and personal disclosure, it is increasingly likely that it will be harder for you to catch all her meaning from words alone. That's where reading between the lines and verifying what you've read come in.

It's not that you have to be a psychic or a private eye to figure out what the heck she's saying, but you will often need to listen as much to what she didn't say as to what she did. Take note of her facial expressions, the words and phrases she characteristically repeats, the topics she seems to specialize in, and the kind of "vibe" as she speaks. All these will help you translate the message from her mind, as it comes through her mouth and into your understanding.

Sometimes it will feel like you're just guessing at what she means or taking a shot in the dark. Sometimes that's exactly what you will be doing. But reading between the lines is more than that, it's using the sum total of what you know about your woman to fill in some of the blanks. Because for you, where understanding increases, so does your ability to express your love and support.

THE BOTTOM LINE

Men at work: Never fill in the blanks in ink until you've checked with her by telling her what you understood her to have meant and allowing her to confirm, clarify, or revise the interpretation. Don't tell her what she meant as if you somehow know that better than she. Tell her what you understand her to have said, and *ask* her if you were on target.

The benefits: Black women long to be heard and understood to the fullest by their men. It's a big part of confirming your devotion to them. You're listening, then going the extra mile to know her well enough to read between the lines and let her sign off on the accuracy of your understanding. It proves to her that you will gladly receive whatever she's giving of herself to you. And that you are even willing to take steps to get more of her.

The costs: Having to read between the lines will sometimes annoy you. On occasion, you'll just plain not feel like having to decode, decipher, and decide what she might have meant.

22. ●◆ *Avoid Analyzing Her to Her*

To the man who loves me:
It's almost like when I was in high school and we had to
examine all kinds of organisms under the microscope and
then had to document all the minute microscopic details
and explain to the class what we had discovered. I'm sure
you don't mean any harm, but I feel as if you are constantly
examining me under a microscope so you can tell me all
about what you've discovered.

—From the Black woman you love

Men absolutely love to get to the bottom of things. They rely heavily on their keen analytical skills to figure out the why of a matter. Arriving at answers to why she is the way she is, why she's saying or doing, desiring or experiencing whatever it is, is not merely for the purpose of satisfying your curiosity about the Black woman you love. You analyze her because it's natural for you to try to break big complex things down into smaller more understandable and thus more manageable pieces. Analyzing her is a man's way of getting meaning and drawing conclusions about what you're hearing and feeling from her. Ultimately, analyzing is what it takes for you to figure out exactly what to do next.

Your woman can have no objections when you're analyzing in the privacy of your own silent thoughts and interpretations. Your thoughts are your business. But when you make it a practice to broadcast the results of your analysis of her to her, you are likely to find she has major problems with that.

I urge you to keep your analysis to yourself and use it for your own benefit in relating to her, rather than offering it, unsolicited, in an attempt to benefit her. Analyzing her to her can make her feel as if she's the subject of your psychological research project and that somehow you now think you're the expert on her. When you try to explain somebody else to them you run the risk of presenting yourself as a more qualified authority on them than they are. Even if your findings happen to be accurate, you could come across as arrogant and judgmental. You are sure to hear her most outraged, "How dare you!" more times than you ever want to.

It doesn't matter how tender your tone or how innocent your intent, you belittle intimacy-building when you start giving her a readout about the "hidden meaning" of her behavior, what her real motives were, or how she is, in fact, experiencing this emotion as opposed to that one. It only causes distance and sets you up as the man of superior knowledge and her as the woman who you've got thoroughly figured out.

THE BOTTOM LINE

Men at work: It's okay to keep your microscope. Analyzing is what men do. But it's best to get rid of your microphone; if she wants to know your take on why she is the way she is she'll ask.

The benefits: If you do your analysis, then keep it to yourself, the woman you love will sense that she is free to unfold who she is and how she is to you. She'll be secure in knowing that she doesn't have to live up to, or explain herself out of, the interpretations that you have made, and shared, all too conclusively with her. It means the world to her that you believe and embrace who she is, not who your analysis has determined, and your pronouncements, declare her to be.

The costs: You may be so good at analyzing people and situations that you are sure that your analysis of her could be helpful to her. You may have to work especially hard to keep your unsolicited analysis from seeping into your conversations with her. It'll feel like a waste of such good insights.

23. ▲ ■ ● ◆ ◗ _Call Her by Name_

To the man who loves me:
I treasure everything you do or could possibly do that
reminds me that I'm yours and you are mine. The sound of
your voice saying my name is one of those little reminders.

—_From the Black woman you love_

The reason clichés become clichés is because they are sayings whose truths are so timeless that they continue to be worth believing and repeating. When you've heard them over and over they can become empty-sounding phrases whose profound, yet simple, lessons can be easily missed because of their boring familiarity. I urge you to give a fresh listen to an old cliché: "In love, it's the little things that count."

One of the "little things" that packs a lot of power in loving a Black woman is for you to call her by name, frequently. It's one of those little things that are really a big thing to the woman you love. Not because she's constantly testing you, to be sure you've not forgotten whether she's a Mary, or a Millie, or a Mabel. Rather it's because women are very fond of the various indications from you that she is *your* Mary, Millie, or Mabel. When her name comes out of your mouth, you symbolically confirm over and over again that she is attached to you, the man who loves her. It can be a revitalizing dose of affirmation that builds her sense of security.

Never be so busy making your point and expressing yourself to her that you give no thought to the "packaging" you put it in. Address her by her name.

None of this means you should repossess those clever, creative, and very private nicknames you've so affectionately given to her. They may have almost become her name to the two of you. She loves them because you chose them, and without even trying to you probably add a certain subtle, flirty, and very intimate flavor to how you say them. Don't stop all that and just call her what's written on her birth certificate and her driver's license. But call her by name, both the ones her mama gave her, and everybody else calls her, as well as the one(s) you created that she just *loves* to answer to.

When you call her by her name, not just "Baby," "Girl," "Sweetheart," or "You" (as in "Hey, You!"), you accomplish two things at once: You of course get her attention *and* you convey in a word that who she is matters to you. That's enough, in the name of love, for you to repeat again and again.

THE BOTTOM LINE

Men at work: Without telling her in advance, work on consistently sprinkling her name (and your most frequently used nicknames) throughout your every conversation with her for a week. Go overboard. When she notices, explain why you are taking care to call her by name.

The benefits: When you consistently practice one of these "little things" that mean so much, the Black woman you love will feel positively adored, which contributes greatly to her self-image as well as her confidence in your love for her. When she feels secure and confident, she is motivated to offer, in return, the kind of loving interaction that matters most to you.

The costs: None, other than the possibility that calling her by name could feel like you're being too stiff and formal, or that it just takes too much time, or that it's too subtle an offering to get you any major applause for doing it. This is a virtually pain-free, risk-free procedure.

24. ▲ ■ ● ◆ ❱ *Touch Her*

To the man who loves me:
Have you ever noticed that little smile on my face when you touch me as you speak? You need to know that, for me, your touch has both tender sweetness and invincible strength in it. It's way beyond skin-deep.

—From the Black woman you love

In loving a Black woman one of your most effective and easily accomplished skills has to do with touch. Of course it's true that women tend to love words and it's probably also true that they want a lot more of them from you. But words can come up short in expressing the kind of closeness, affection, approval, affirmation, tenderness, desire, reassurance, devotion, and concern that touching her can. Black women cherish their men's gentle touch.

I'm talking here about your basic, uncomplicated, reach-out-and-touch. Caressing, stroking, and fondling are fine and not to be avoided in the appropriate context. But I'm attempting to sell you on the liberal use of "plain wrap," generic touch. Women know that when you touch them, especially spontaneously and unsolicited, you momentarily interrupt all that momentum propelling you toward your next project, obligation, or destination. When you touch them as you speak or listen or think, they, for that moment, *become* your cherished project. They feel elevated to a singular place of honor among all the things that matter to you.

But how much touch and when and how exactly she wants it are questions that loom large in the mind of an action-oriented man. To get the answers you'll have to ask and experiment.

No two Black women are exactly alike in their capacity and their appreciation for touch. For some, a little here and a little there go a long way. For others, there's no such thing as too much. You'll need to adjust the measure and your methods according to the feedback you get from her.

Unfortunately, some Black women, maybe even the one you love, have experienced the indignity of being mishandled, through physical and sexual abuse, and other violations of their bodies, minds, and souls. For them physical displays of affection, sometimes even simple touch, can feel intrusive and undesirable. Don't take it personally if she is not as receptive to your touch as you would like. Best to let her request more of it than to give more than she can comfortably handle.

THE BOTTOM LINE

Men at work: Nearly anytime reach out and tenderly touch the side of her face, her shoulders, hips, or hands as you converse. Keep it light and nonsexual. From time to time ask her if she's getting enough touch (or too much). Adjust accordingly. Experiment, ask, adjust.

The benefits: When you touch her as you speak, she'll surely be more attentive to you and what you're saying. Touch often effectively conveys through your hands what's in your heart that may be hard to put into words. Your touch will constantly reconfirm, nonverbally, that she is a valuable treasure in your world.

The costs: It may take some work for you to alter your natural style in order to touch your mate more. In some cases your woman will be uncomfortable with the amount of touch you give. So not only won't you be shown the major appreciation you'd like, you could be asked to tone it down or cut it out.

25. ▲ ♦ *Do Your Best, Then Be Yourself*

To the man who loves me:
If it has ever seemed like I've required you to become some-body that you're not in order to live up to my fantasy, for-give me. And if you've ever fallen for it and tried to become my fantasies, I forgive you.

—From the Black woman you love

Even if you are truly a good man, you'll never be a perfect one. As you work hard to live up to your highest potential, you'll find that at various points along the way you will both disgust and impress yourself and the Black woman you love.

There's nothing sorrier than the sight of a man who has stopped trying to become something more and better than he was yesterday. A better husband, lover, father, friend. A better leader, servant, or team player. A better human being.

But as valid as it is that you keep striving to become more excellent, you must pay close attention to your goal. If you're attempting to live out the best of your unique identity authentically and honorably, you'll try to perform in every area of your life to the best of your ability, consistently doing the most you can, with what you've got. But if your goal is to become (or appear to become) everything she may fantasize her man should be, then your goal isn't worth very much.

A loving relationship with a Black woman should never mean you give up the perfectly legitimate elements of who you are (and how you are) to match her (or anyone else's) unrealistic notions. Often women, especially those who during their childhoods didn't have the benefit of ever-present, real-life models of manhood from their fathers, develop a pronounced hunger for masculine love. It's a legitimate hunger, but one that has been distorted by unrealistic ideas about the package it should come in. She may be completely unaware that what she expects and requires from the man in her life is way beyond what is reasonable and is closer to myth, legend, or wishful thinking.

Add to that the fact that men can easily fall prey to the performance-driven, approval-seeking temptation to fulfill those fantasies. It's an attempt to gain applause and the self-esteem perks that go with it. It's also a setup for disaster. Offer her who you are, not the fantasy role she may cast you in.

Though you may possess certain of the fantasy role's qualities, you are not, nor do you ever need to become, her knight in shining armor, her stern but loving father, or her smooth-talking leading man, her twenty-four-hour delivery boy, or "the one who will make me complete." It's not your place to be all that, and if you act as if it is, you'll be disgusted with yourself. Efforts at fantasy fulfillment do major damage. They invite shallow, unsatisfying relationships that are based on what one or both of you think you ought to be, rather than what you are. There's no way to keep it real under these conditions. That's why so many Black women and their men end up throwing each other away, only to begin the long wait and the endless search all over again.

THE BOTTOM LINE

Men at work: Stop and carefully consider the most consistent desires, requests, expectations, and "requirements" your woman expresses to you—especially the ones you seem to keep failing to fulfill. Were they realistic in the first place or have they emerged from her or your fantasies and unrealistic notions about what a good man is or does? Whenever you suspect it's fantasy, discuss it with her honestly and plainly. Let her know what she realistically can expect in your personality, your performance, and what you have to offer her in the relationship. It's up to her to revise her fantasy. It's up to you to work to give the very best of yourself to her—authentically and sincerely—no more, no less.

The benefits: When you boldly offer your woman the things that make you, you, it will do away with much disillusionment and disappointment between the two of you down the road. You'll bring the measure of your love and commitment down to the realistic, the achievable, and available. Which means you can give and she can finally receive real-life love from the real-life man in her life. Not an often impressive, but inconsistent, fake.

The costs: If you believe women are always the most qualified experts on loving relationships you may have a hard time turning down her fantasy as your goal. You're apt to believe that her fantasy-filled expectations are valid. And that to challenge them, or fail to live up to them, is wrong. You can expect feelings of failure and dissatisfaction under these circumstances.

26. ▲ ■ ● *Own Up to and Express Your Fears*

To the man who loves me:
Your whole life is important to me, including the things that make you afraid. I don't care how courageous you look, every-body feels some fear sometimes. I can only assume that you do too, because you don't go there with me. I wish you would.

—From the Black woman you love

Being a good man is very hard work. Focus, sensitivity, courage, wisdom, and ingenuity are the necessary ingredients if you are to accomplish all that you and the Black woman you love are counting on you for. If you are succeeding at loving her, taking care of yourself, and seeing to the myriad responsibilities of a man's life you probably feel like you're juggling a hundred plates at one time—and any minute all of them could come crashing to the floor. Even if you are extremely proud about how well you're doing, life and love can be intimidating.

Fear is a natural part of living. Those who succeed at anything big, do so in spite of fear. Not because they had none. Fear of failure, fear of loss, fear of powerlessness, ineffectiveness, being mistaken, misunderstood, or ignored. Fear that you will never achieve what you aspired to, and fear that you will fail to maintain what you have achieved. Fear is common to both men and women; neither has a monopoly on it. But when it comes to acknowledging and expressing fear, men, especially when in the presence of their women, can have a particularly hard time. That's unfortunate because Black women crave the opportunity to share in all that's hidden inside you. Sadly, your fears are inaccessible to them if you hide, deny, or call them something other than what they are.

The easiest trick in the world is to camouflage your fears. Rather than admitting that there is some anxiety, self-doubt, intimidation, embarrassment, or some other kind of fear troubling you, you opt to hide it by expressing what seems more acceptably masculine: anger, indifference, blame, or sarcasm. When you do that she can easily get the impression that you are not so much a fearless, unshakable model of masculinity, but that you are a selfish soul who's out of touch with his feelings and who therefore couldn't possibly handle hers very well.

Owning up to your fears means you are the kind of person who is well balanced and emotionally secure enough to refuse to measure yourself by some ridiculous macho stereotype. You're the kind of man she can bring her love, support, and encouragement to and know you'll accept it. When she's not allowed that, the relationship sorely misses the mark to her. It's emptier and less fulfilling than one where she is valued as the person to whom you can show the bitter and the sweet of your insides because you're man enough to own up to and express your fears.

THE BOTTOM LINE

Men at work: When you are aware of feeling tense, angry, embarrassed, or anxious, try to identify the origin of those feelings. Do they involve something between you and your woman, or some other facet of your life? Boldly, honestly access the degree to which some fear, uncertainty, or insecurity is really what's bothering you. Acknowledge and (when appropriate) admit your fears to your woman rather than keep them stuffed in by employing rage, finger-pointing, frozen silence, or feigned indifference to camouflage them.

The benefits: You can gain her support, encouragement, and understanding when you need it most. She gets the fulfilling opportunity to share one more part of your world that she has previously been barred from. You'll not waste so much time and energy hiding from your fears or deflecting them onto the woman you love or something else.

The costs: Taking the risk of a new level of vulnerability and the possibility that she'll condemn your fearful feelings as a sign of weakness. Or that she'll make the mistake of trying to take control of your life, to rid it of any of its potential risks.

27. ▲ ■ ● ◆ ◗ *Let Her Know When You're Headed Underground*

To the man who loves me:
To me, being in this thing with you is all about us giving each other what we need in order to be at our best. It seems there are times when you really need me to be patient with you and willing to wait. I'm willing to give you that. But I need you to let me know when that is what you need from me.

—From the Black woman you love

Women can have a very hard time with the secrets men keep. Even if you're not intentionally trying to keep a secret, your brooding silences, unexplained mood changes, and eternal "everything's okay" responses can be mysterious and frustrating to her. She experiences them as unclimbable walls and uncrossable miles that separate the two of you.

All she has to go on is the knowledge that when women have anxious concerns, nagging questions, or important decisions to deal with they tend to want to talk them out with each other. So she'll tend to try, immediately or repeatedly, to make that happen with you. And immediately and repeatedly she'll find that it just doesn't work that way.

Partnering together around deeply emotional issues is completely natural to them and greatly appreciated. She may not know that men don't do it that way. In fact, what sends her to a "talk it out" partner to dialogue, discuss, and decide usually sends men into private thought and silent contemplation. One style is no better or worse than the other as long as eventually the processing and reporting back with each other happens.

But unless you tell her otherwise, she is likely to assume that when you descend into your "underground" where you temporarily kick back, zone out, and shut down (so you can process your feelings) it will feel to her like you've suddenly hung up the phone on her in the middle of a lively conversation.

For the sake of her feelings and your need for some quiet solitude to figure out how you're feeling, why you're feeling it, and what to do about it, tell her when you're headed underground. Do it honestly, do it simply, do it unapologetically—just make sure you do it. Otherwise, she won't be sure what your silence means and at first she'll struggle with the feeling that something's wrong and she is somehow at fault. Then she'll ache to know what she can do to heal the separation; and because you're deep in the silence of your underground (and because it's not about her anyway) she won't get answers. And then she'll really be thrown off and tempted to demand you break your silence—immediately! Or she'll offer you her silence in return. It's a nasty little process that can be short-circuited at the outset if you let her know that your travel plans include an immediate trip underground. But always round-trip, not one way.

THE BOTTOM LINE

Men at work: When you need the time and freedom for some private processing, warn her in advance by saying something like "I've got some figuring out to do, I'm headed underground. When I've got a handle on it, I'll be back and I'll let you in on it."

The benefits: Informing your woman before you head underground frees you to take the time you need to process, analyze, and clarify your thoughts and feelings. Promising to return to her with your findings makes it clear to her that you aren't trying to shut her out. In fact, you're doing what you need to do to be able to include her.

The costs: No man wants to feel as if he has to "get permission" to be alone with his own thoughts. But the fact is, it may be difficult getting the downtime you need to figure out your feelings if you don't clarify what your apparent withdrawal does and does not mean.

28. ▲ ■ ● ◆) *Tolerate Her Rambling*

To the man who loves me:
Would you just let me make my point. If I take five minutes, or five years, to do it, I'd really appreciate it if you'd just let me make my point my way.

—From the Black woman you love

One of the key ways women respond to the complications of life and love is to talk. For women, sharing, relating, and dialoguing help them to clarify and process what they feel, what they think, and what they need to do. The Black woman in your life, or the one on the way, will naturally tend to think out loud, and in the company of someone else who cares. The more emotion-laden the issue, the more she'll need to talk to be able to successfully respond to it. Like it or not, she'll most want to talk with you.

Though you may be the sensitive, caring, gracious kind of

man who welcomes his woman to share her heart and bare her soul, you may soon find her words too long and your patience and attention span too short. At those times, you'll need to sit tight and tolerate what will sound to you like pure rambling repetition with no bottom line in sight. Your heart will beat faster. You'll grow restless and your brain will begin to feel overworked and underpaid. In spite of it all, for her sake, you'll need to tolerate her rambling. In fact, you'll be even more helpful to her if you encourage her to keep on talking until she's talked it through and figured it out.

There are few things that rate higher on a woman's list of what a "good man" does than affirming her by listening to her and giving her room to explore her feelings with you without having to put it all in alphabetical order and without it being concise, articulate, practical, or profound (i.e., just the way men like it to be when they speak or when they have to listen!).

THE BOTTOM LINE

Men at work: Be receptive to her talking through what she's going through with you. Allow her to move in and around the issues in her own possibly "all over the place" style. Offer your woman your interested, attentive body language, as well as verbal encouragement (like questions that prove you're listening, comments that express your understanding and empathy for her feelings, and summarizing her message back to her in her words) while keeping any unsolicited advice to yourself.

The benefits: If you'll tolerate her rambling and even lend her your verbal as well as nonverbal assistance to help her keep talking, you'll witness her ability to work out her own difficulties quite ably. Then you won't have to struggle with feeling you must take on the burdens and responsibility of "fixing" her life. You'll find her self-sufficiency very attractive and she'll be captivated by your sensitivity and your acceptance of her and her style of processing issues.

The costs: Your urge to get as quickly as possible to a logical, concrete conclusion can make listening to her circular, detail-filled, and not necessarily goal-oriented discourse unbearable at times. You'll have to put up with the blood-pressure-raising reality that to employ your analytical, advice-dispensing, "get on with it" style is only likely to cause her to shut down, detach, and get the support and affirmation she needs the way she needs it—elsewhere.

29. ▲ ● ◆ *Never Run from Her Tears*

To the man who loves me:
I understand my tears can be a problem for you. I wish they weren't. I wish your heart would stop beating so fast and your body wasn't so tense when I'm crying in your arms. Without even trying to, I usually count to see how many seconds will pass before you let go of me and leave me to cry alone.

—From the Black woman you love

Women cry. Some only rarely, others quite frequently. Most of them understand that the shedding of tears is a perfectly acceptable and highly effective response to a wide range of emotions, including, but certainly not limited to, disappointment, joy, fear, anger, surprise, and fatigue. Contrary to what you may think, her tears are not a signal that you are expected to solve something for her. That's a burden that could make you want to run for your life. So relax and don't check out on her. You needn't run from her tears.

A good sincere cry is her body's way of paying tribute to what has already deeply touched her heart and soul. It's one of the most natural and honest human expressions. Though the Black woman you love expends effort and energy doing it, her tears are not meant to solve, settle, or signify anything. For her, crying is 100 percent genuine present-tense feeling. No more than that, and no less. Your best bet in loving her is to give her the space to feel and express what she's experiencing without running the risk that you'll soon be plotting your escape. You don't have to punch a time card, roll up your sleeves, and get busy working to get her all dry and happy again.

When she cries, men who are big on "doing," and "undoing," for their women often struggle with the suspicion that a) You messed up something, and she wants you to undo it; b) She messed up something, and she wants you to take care of her by taking care of it; or c) She has a baffling situation or decision and she wants you to solve it.

Warning: You can be so distracted by this guilt and feeling of responsibility that you can't tune in and support her fully in what she's going through. Lonely for her. Even if there are issues that need to be fixed, for the sake of the woman you love, don't shift so fast into fix-it mode. Avoid saying or doing anything, especially with an expression on your face that says you find her tears immature or inappropriate. At those moments don't play her psychologist, fairy godfather, or the voice of reason. Instead, give her your patience and your listening ears (and your crying eyes if you've got them). It's definitely not the time for you to work on being more verbal with her. The worst thing you could do is withdraw mentally, physically, or emotionally from her tears.

THE BOTTOM LINE

Men at work: Offer your concern, your patience, and your presence when she is emotional to the point of tears. Fight the urge to take blame or feel guilt for her feelings (unless you really are to blame). Focus on her. Don't silence her or try to fix her when you can hold her and just wait it out. Use everything you've got that confirms to her that you understand how she could feel the way she feels.

The benefits: When you refuse to detach from her and her tears, you put the "gentle" in "gentleman." She'll absolutely flourish knowing she has the kind of man who can silently, tenderly, patiently practice emotional intimacy rather than abandon her in response to her tears.

The costs: You may experience that awkward, impotent feeling that comes when you believe you should be doing something but you're not sure what, and you're not sure it would do any good anyway.

30. ▲ ■ ● ◆) *Remind Her Daily of Why You Love Her*

To the man who loves me:
There are some things I only need you to say or do once and that's enough. The benefit will last forever. But telling me about your love for me is something I can never get too much of.

—From the Black woman you love

God knows you've got your reasons for loving the Black woman in your life. But does that woman know? I mean really *know,* not suspect, hope, or assume. Today, at this very second, does she know beyond a shadow of a doubt how much you love her and why? If you're counting on her knowing because of the wonderful words you uttered, or the things you did yesterday, don't. Today is a brand-new day. She could use some new reminders. Best to act as if every one of yesterday's reminders and reassurances expired and need to be replaced with a fresh supply.

You can never tell the Black woman you love how much you love her and why, too much. If your declarations are sincere and flow steadily, even if they are a little repetitious, you nourish her soul and firm up the very foundation of the relationship: her assurance that you unconditionally love her and day by day you choose to continue. Constant daily reaffirmations of that fact speak peace to that part of a woman that is prone to struggle with self-doubts and insecurity about your love and commitment. Those nagging doubts and insecurities are just as real and normal as yours are about your abilities and accomplishments.

Whatever your feelings about her and commitment to her may be, the reality is you have made a willing choice to love her. It was not an accident or an involuntary reflex. Yours is a deliberate decision based on an assortment of whys and wherefores. Every day go out of your way to remind her and yourself of what they are.

Is it because of her strong but gentle and nurturing spirit? Is it the faith she has in you and the supportive, respectful way she shows it? Is it her one in a million outer packaging and her even more phenomenal inner beauty? Is it the wisdom with which she speaks and her knowing use of silence? Or is it her iron-willed determination and infinite patience? Maybe it's the flirty sway of her hips as she walks toward you, the way she never fails to pray for you or the way it feels when she gently strokes your face. Is it any of these? Maybe all of these and much more. Whatever they are, they are hugely important to her. Important enough for you to remind her of them every day.

THE BOTTOM LINE

Men at work: Never be so busy building a future together that you fail to revisit the reason that you loved her in the first place. Simply tell her out of nowhere, making use of those unscheduled moments you have together. Turn to her and say, "I love you so much because you . . ." Whether you write it, phone it, fax it, e-mail it, or sing it out loud, remind her constantly.

The benefits: Your daily reassuring reminders of why you love her are your most practical and effective strategies for communicating your desire for her and commitment to her. It's how you can contribute to keeping her doubt and insecurity level low and her faith in you and your love high.

The costs: It may feel like a bothersome daily obligation that will get old fast. Deep on the inside you'd rather she just know you love her today and every day until you tell her otherwise. The possibility also exists that when you tell her she won't appear to make a big deal of it. Believe me, if you sincerely mean what you say, it will be a big deal to her, whether she shows it or not.

31. ■ ◆ *Be Willing to Sacrifice Your Schedule for Her*

To the man who loves me:
I know you have a million and one things to deal with every
day. I can understand that. I do too and believe me I'm not
trying to get you to stop taking care of business. But those
times when you shift your obligations around or cancel
something just so you can be with me mean so much to me.
I treasure those times.

—From the Black woman you love

Black women are born with a built-in nurture radar that makes them alert to how they can make someone else's life easier, more comfortable, and more secure by their sacrifice. They are willing to do it for all those they deeply care about, including their children, friends, co-workers, and the men in their lives. They are no strangers to the expression of love and commitment through self-sacrifice. Their giving to us frequently involves giving up something for us. They've usually done it willingly with few regrets, but they've noticed how their sacrifice has richly blessed our lives. They long to bask in the warmth of your sacrifices on their behalf as well.

What sends the most persuasive love message to her is when you show a willingness to sometimes sacrifice what you cherish most. Women know men cherish their schedules dearly. We men tend to be inherently goal-oriented and masters of the outer world with all its ambitions, pursuits, deadlines, and limited time constraints. We thrive on knowing what we've got to do, having what it takes to do it, and getting it done as quickly and perfectly as possible. Our schedules are our efficient ways to organize what we cherish most—accomplishments. Accomplishment is what it's all about for men.

You freshly, powerfully affirm her worth to you when you temporarily toss off the demands of the outer world and in the name of love give in to a delay, temporary shutdown, or hiatus. It's giving her a portion of the time that you already had scheduled for conquering new worlds, in order to spend time with the Black woman you love pursuing a richer inner world of intimacy.

Sacrificing your schedule says to her that you are indeed very busy and that you are available to her in spite of that fact. It means a lot when she asks for the sacrifice and you grant it. It means even more when you grant it without being asked. It may be as little as your regular everyday half-a-second kiss being expanded to a long passionate embrace, or making an unscheduled (an uncharacteristic) "hey how's your day going" phone call. Or as much as sacrificing one of your normal basketball, bowling, or "by yourself" days to spend in her company. Or a last-minute vacation together at the height of your busy season. You'll know you are right in the zone when it feels like you are sacrificing your time for something in which little concrete and result-rich is happening.

Your willingness to slow down your life for her (truly willing counts even when you are not truly able) brings relief to the parts of her that have been wounded by things like the discouraging ratio of Black women to Black men, the feeling of being ignored or coming up short compared to women of other races, body types, skin and hair types, and so on. It's an action-oriented, creative way of loving her that "speaks" of your esteem for her. Though nonverbally expressed, it speaks loud and clear.

THE BOTTOM LINE

Men at work: Be specific. Tell her how much or how little time you have. And, great or small, give it to her with your undivided attention. Don't be afraid that if you do it once she'll begin to require more than you can afford to give.

The benefits: Ironically, when she is confident of your willingness to sacrifice your schedule, she will be less compelled to make "test" requests for it. That's the nature of sacrifice: It gives based on what will bless someone you love today, not what it might cost you tomorrow.

The costs: Efficiency, productivity, and the powerful sense of control that strict schedule-keeping affords you may be jeopardized by sacrificing in this way.

32. ■ ● ◆ *Follow Her Lead Sometimes*

To the man who loves me:
I really appreciate it when you are secure enough to
acknowledge that sometimes you don't know the way. I
appreciate it even more when you are willing to go with me
when I do know the way.

—From the Black woman you love

The way the Black woman in your life got to be in your life at all is because you saw in her some impressive qualities and characteristics. She possessed some strengths and virtues that made you sit up and take notice. Doubtless you discovered that owing to her background, her experiences, her interests, education, or God-given ability there are some things in which she is more expert than you. It could be in managing the checkbook, setting the schedule, organizing the project, disciplining the children, closing the deal, or any one of countless other things. If she's demonstrated she's got more interest and effectiveness, you'd both be foolish not to follow her lead in that area.

You've got your strengths, she's got hers. Wisdom requires that you both become good at leading and following according to your abilities, interests, and expertise rather than based on tired stereotypes that require men to know it all and lead the way in order to maintain their masculine honor. With that kind of foolish setup, women, in order to be considered respectful and submissive, are only expected to take the lead when it comes to cooking, cleaning, or raising the kids.

The very strengths which you first admired and appreciated in her, her resourcefulness, her know-how in specific areas, or her competent approach to the tasks at hand, can, if you don't watch out, quickly become unappreciated and ignored by you. It can be hard to follow her lead if you feel that relying upon her expertise means you're not living up to what it means to be a man. In addition, when women perform functions effectively they are gratified by knowing that their efforts contributed to the betterment of an entity larger than themselves, as in the relationship, their family, their team, their organization. It's a part of the natural relational dynamic that pervades the feminine psyche.

Each time she is hindered or not allowed to make use of her full resources and abilities, for the benefit of the two of you together, a little piece of what motivates and fulfills her is snuffed out. It's a tragic and unnecessary waste. To say nothing of the loss to you and that thing that needed to be taken care of by somebody in the know.

When you submit to her lead sometimes, she gets to see that you recognize, value, and rely upon her unique strength. If you don't, she'll feel like she's a stranger that you've never taken the time to get to know. That's a million miles away from where she wants to stand in your eyes.

THE BOTTOM LINE

Men at work: Confess to yourself and your mate areas in which you have stubbornly resisted following her lead. Work on changing your mind-set. Ask her to let you know when she feels you are holding back or taking over in that area again. Above all, point out to her the areas of her knowledge, ability, and skill that you recognize and respect.

The benefits: Acknowledging her expertise and following her lead is yet another extremely powerful way you testify to her as to what you find desirable and impressive about her. In this way you again answer that all-important question: "Why do you love me?"

The costs: If in any way your masculine identity was tied to always being the one who leads and having a woman who meekly follows, becoming more role-flexible here may be a painfully ego-crushing experience.

33. ▲ ■ ● ◆ ◗ Initiate Physical Affection That Doesn't Always Lead to Sex

To the man who loves me:
There is a way you hold and kiss me that makes me feel as if
you're giving me a very special gift that's for me and me only.
Then there are other times when your touches and kisses feel
to me like they're mainly for you to get something from me
for yourself. I think you should know that when I get enough
of the first kind I can enjoy more of the second kind.

—From the Black woman you love

If the Black woman you love gets the idea that every time
you display affection by hugging, kissing, holding, tender talk,
and gentle caressing you are leading up to having sex, you
might become confused and annoyed at how unwelcome
your affection becomes to her. Women tend to be suspicious
of love play if it always turns out to have been foreplay.

Though she may have a healthy appetite and appreciation for you and for sex, she wants very much to be sure
that's not all or even mostly what makes her desirable to you.
Typically, women view sex as something that they do, a
meaningful, beautiful, delicious thing they do to express their
love, but it's not an expression of their identities. For you to
desire the pleasure of her sexuality doesn't necessarily mean
to her that you deeply desire her as a person. Sex makes the
most sense and holds the most value to her when she has
the deep assurance that outside of sex she is already cherished, approved of, and delighted in. When you initiate physical expressions of your affection for her and consistently

demonstrate sex is not required, she begins to believe what can sometimes be hard for her to believe, that you truly value her for her sake. Not just for the sake of the physical pleasure she can make you feel.

THE BOTTOM LINE

Men at work: Frequently initiate affectionate, physical expressions like hand-holding, passionate kisses and embraces, caressing, and cuddling that are nongenital, non-sexual, and appropriate to the commitment level of your relationship. Don't let her have to initiate all nonsexual displays of affection and you initiate all the sexual ones.

The benefits: There is a bond of closeness and comfort that comes from your nonsexual affection that can only be gotten there. You make it clear that she doesn't have to "give it up" to be able to receive love from you. Ironically, when you offer sincere physical affection that doesn't lead to sex, you are likely to find her even more responsive to your sexual advances.

The costs: As a man, her sexual desire and the expression of it means as much to you as your nonsexual affection does to her. You may sometimes feel frustrated and a bit deprived by stimulating love play that doesn't find its release in sex. That kind of sacrifice can be costly to you, yet tremendously rewarding to the woman you love.

34. ■ ● ◆ ❯ *Share Your Insides with Her*

To the man who loves me:
I want to know you so much. What I see on the outside pleases
me no end. Come on now, take me further. Tell me what I
don't see. Show me your heart.

—From the Black woman you love

She really wants to know you literally inside and out. She wants to know the past, present, and future of your experiences, your thoughts, and your desires and what you're absolutely assured of and what completely baffles you. She wants to know your feelings, motives, and fears, and the way the world looks through your eyes. Knowing the entire inventory of your heart, mind, and soul matters to her far more than you may imagine. And she'll work hard, some men complain too hard, to gain access to your private inner world and get the treasures that are stored there.

Her need to know should not be taken as a sign that she is just plain nosy; she's probably not "fishing" so she can use the information she gains to back you into a commitment corner. It's not her attempt to unearth some good reasons to criticize or condemn you. She is on a search expedition because women feel freest to give the best of their love and themselves to the man they know thoroughly—from the inside out. It is only when she feels secure that she knows you (not just the historical facts about you) that she feels truly connected to you in secure love and intimacy.

Knowing your insides has a lot riding on it for her. The best move you could make is to not only invite her into your private world, but to take the initiative to reveal that rich part of you to her on purpose rather than to make it a restricted area with limited access and a "don't ask, don't tell" policy.

As challenging and unnatural as it may seem to commit to sharing your insides with her, you do it by:

- Not waiting for her to ask how your day went, but from time to time offering her all the boring details before she requests them.
- Taking the time you may need to process your thoughts and feelings about an issue between the two of you and coming back to share those feelings without her having to make repeated requests.
- Relaxing your compulsion with keeping your business to yourself at all cost.
- Refusing to buy into the unnecessary requirement that the length, style, and content of your sharing has to match hers. Be thorough, but do it your way.
- Incorporating specific emotion words (like sad, glad, discouraged, enthusiastic, angry, intimidated, embarrassed) into your self-disclosure rather than only hinting at or completely hiding your actual feelings.

THE BOTTOM LINE

Men at work: Take the woman you love on a guided tour of your private inner world. Work on sharing yourself by your honest and thorough verbal expression. You'll get better at talking about yourself by choosing to do it, and she'll get better at listening to you, understanding and accepting you, by having to.

The benefits: It keeps her desire to love alive. When women don't get access to your private thoughts, feelings, and experiences—your inner world—their sense of a vital, secure bond of intimacy with you is lacking. She's likely, then, to "go through the motions" in the relationship, only offering and expecting in return a frail, superficial love.

The costs: The vulnerability and awkwardness of sharing more than you feel like sharing and the risk that she'll misunderstand, judge, or attempt to change you when you do share your inner self.

35. ▲ *Expect to Love Her Out of Both Desire and Duty*

To the man who loves me:
You continue to offer me the very best of your love, even when our feelings for each other are not at their best. I am grateful that your love is so sturdy and determined.

—From the Black woman you love

If all your images of what love is come from sexy R&B ballads, Hollywood movies, the pages of fiction, lies from the locker room, or your favorite recurring daydream, you're likely to believe that real love is just a feeling: passion. But if that's your working definition of love, you'll require that it always flow from your passion all the time and when your passion grows thin so will your love. That's unfortunate and unnecessary.

Love and passion are not the same thing. Passion is only a fringe benefit of love, a fabulous, though often temporary, emotion that, just like Christmas, comes and goes and can come and go again.

But real-life love is fueled by discipline and duty far more than by passionate feelings. Though discipline carries more weight and substance than passionate desire does, passion has discipline and duty beat when it comes to exhilarating feelings.

Sadly, we live in a feelings-obsessed culture where if you're not careful you'll be sucked into believing that when the feelings are not intense neither is the love. That ain't necessarily so!

Accept the fact that ongoing love for the Black woman in your life will emerge from your disciplined commitment and desire. You simply don't always have to feel so lovey-dovey to be able to love her and be loved in return. Don't require it.

Passionate desire, intoxicated romantic feelings of being "in love" with your woman are like the waves of the sea, they flow in and they flow back out again. You really don't have as much control over your feelings as you may think you do. They can change like the weather. The "how you feel" part of love is constantly based on a million things that may or may not be going on in your life, her life, or your love life together. Believe me, whether the passion is at high tide or low, *this too shall pass*. No need to sweat this fact. Enjoy it when intense desire is present, remain disciplined and committed when it's not.

Discipline is the willful choice to do what love requires without needing that it be fueled by the energizing thrust of your passionate feelings. Discipline continues to speak words of love and perform acts of love because discipline has fought and won the battle to keep love from being enslaved to our constantly shifting feelings.

Love that doesn't guarantee the uninterrupted presence of passion, fierce attraction, total compatibility, and constant positive feelings may sound dull and dreary. It needn't be at all, because if you keep working at the disciplines of love—respect, affection, sacrifice, and patience—they will sustain you through the comings and goings of your waves of passion.

THE BOTTOM LINE

Men at work: Stop evaluating the worth and overall rightness of your relationship based on less significant factors like feeling "in love," maintaining "want-to feelings," 24/7, or other vague on-again, off-again variables. Chemistry, compatibility, electricity, and passion are not all true love is about. Consider your love, and hers, to be acceptable when it flows from "choose to" rather than "want to."

The benefits: Your willingness to commit to constant love without requiring constant passion is the best safeguard against needlessly throwing away a potentially great relationship (especially a marriage). When you take your feelings down from the number-one priority spot, you become less vulnerable to the oppressive perfectionism that can keep you starting and ending relationships merely based on the rise and fall of your emotions.

The costs: You may feel like a hypocrite acting lovingly toward your woman based on your willful choice and your discipline rather than spontaneous desire. However, to act in accordance with your true identity—as her *committed* lover—is not hypocritical, it's consistent.

36. ▲ ■ ● ◆ ）
Protect Her

To the man who loves me:
I've been watching over my shoulder and peeping around
corners to look out for myself for so long that I almost didn't
notice that you're right here with me. I need your strength
and your concern for me and for my well-being. When I
have them I feel even safer.

—From the Black woman you love

It's not that you have to be the Man of Steel because she's
a frightened and defenseless little girl in harm's way. In fact,
Black women have stood tall and fared well, going toe-to-toe
against some of life's most threatening adversaries. They have
victoriously withstood savage exploitation, cruel injustice, bitter loneliness, and violent abuses against their own physical
and emotional well-being, and against their families. They are
fighters and often they are conquerors. Yet none of this takes
away from the fact that she deeply desires that you care
enough about her to protect her.

Don't be fooled by her confident, "take no mess" exterior,
the hardness of her speech, and the boldness with which she
responds to a challenge. Your woman has probably learned to
deal with those who would harm her, alone and as best she
could, because too often she had to, not because she wanted
to. She'd love for you to join her and in many cases to assume
the responsibility of protecting her. She wants to relax in the
assurance that you won't easily tolerate those who would
speak to her disrespectfully, strike, mishandle or threaten her,
or otherwise act with malicious intent. If she's the woman you

love, she longs to know beyond a shadow of a doubt that you've got her back.

To protect her may sometimes only mean that you show up with her, proving that she's not just a woman alone, she's connected to a man who treasures her, and who will protect what he treasures, by any means necessary. At other times, it may mean that you'll have to discreetly, but firmly, confront those who step over the line with her. Whether it's a smart-mouthed cashier or a drunken fool in the streets—or in your own living room! At all times protecting her will mean taking care that you are never the one who disrespects or demeans her by your own words or deeds.

THE BOTTOM LINE

Men at work: Take a position and respond with the necessary show of force to those who in any way pose a threat or have mistreated your woman. Keep ego and showmanship out of it. Protect her for the sake of her sense of security. Resist the natural inclination to ignore or minimize what she sees as threatening. Even if you think it's something she can and should take the lead in handling, let her know why you do, then walk supportively with her as she handles the issue.

The benefits: To be protective of the woman you love demonstrates to her that you take her security and well-being seriously. You make it clear that she is not alone in this world. She knows that men fiercely defend and protect what matters most to them.

The costs: You definitely won't be able to take away all threats, risks, and dangers from her life even though you may feel you should. In fact, some of what feels threatening to her will feel that way to you as well. Stir up your courage and do the best you can. Also, there will be areas of her life in which she doesn't need, or want, your protection. In fact, she may resent your attempts to handle challenging problems or people that she wants to handle herself. You'll have to rely on your instincts and her feedback to learn which kind are which.

37. ♠♦ *Be Conservative in the Promises You Make*

To the man who loves me:
When you promise me you'll do this, that, or the other, I admit I'm thrilled at first. But promising me the world is not necessary if you're not absolutely sure you're going to keep those promises.

—*From the Black woman you love*

Since the Black woman you love doesn't have X-ray vision and she can't read your mind or accurately predict the future, she has to gauge some pretty important internal things about you, as in your character and commitment, by observing some external indicators. Perhaps none of your externals are more telling than the promises you make and your record at keeping them.

When you get right down to it, the way you handle promises is the vital indicator to your woman of how much or how little of her trust she can safely bestow upon you. There has probably never been a time in the history of the world when Black women have more yearned to be able to trust the men in their lives. Sadly, some of her deepest wounds and most crushing disappointments were because of someone's broken promises to her.

Simple, consistent promise-keeping will always be more meaningful to her than fancy, overzealous promise-making. Making few promises but following through on the ones you make will dramatically increase the level of her trust and security. But to make an abundance of promises—even well-intentioned ones—and only keep a few counts for little and in fact will eventually erode her trust in you and her respect for you over time. When it comes to promises, you're always better off a conservative rather than a liberal.

Instead of putting your lofty dreams, appealing possibilities, and extravagant ambitions into the form of promises you make to her, come down to the more earthly commitments that you already have the desire and the ability to keep. Otherwise your promise is only a maybe. Maybes are great as personal goals, but they are lousy as oaths to someone else. A commitment to conservative promise-making and consistent promise-keeping should apply to all matters—across the board. From as serious as the promise to marry her, down to the promise to pick her up at 7:00, not 7:30 or 8:00.

THE BOTTOM LINE

Men at work: Only promise what you mean to perform and can perform. If something unforeseen and uncontrollable delays or prevents you from keeping your word, don't assume she'll know that. Take the initiative to offer an explanation— and an apology. Note: You can always go ahead and do incredibly impressive and much appreciated things for her without having made a promise to do them.

The benefits: When you make few promises and keep the ones you make, you set a high standard of integrity and sensitivity in your relationship. The woman you love won't have to wonder about the weight of your words or the worth of your character. You won't have to spend your life constantly defending, justifying, and explaining why you broke your promises.

The costs: You give up the strategic use of overly extravagant promise-making as a means of impressing, consoling, or manipulating her. You may have to work hard to find other ways to accomplish those goals.

38. *Never Beg*

To the man who loves me:
My brother, please get up off your knees. You don't belong there and I can't stand to watch you do that to yourself.

—From the Black woman you love

Maybe you do need to work on being less demanding, harsh, stubborn, loud, or any number of other "mannish" ways of being. Finding the proper balance in how you relate to the Black woman in your life is crucial. You obviously want to, or you wouldn't have made it this far in this book, but even if you are on a mission to tone down, mellow out, and soften the edges of your style, never let that tempt you to become a man who begs.

Begging is the desperate, humiliating extreme side of requesting. When you beg you throw off your dignity and your self-sufficiency to plead for your woman to give you what you want, how and when you want it. Men who beg think too highly of her (she's a woman, after all, not a goddess) and they think too little of themselves.

Begging your woman for anything, whether it's approval, understanding, money, time, freedom, sex, or whatever else, is a big-time setup for disaster. When you make it obvious that you see yourself in dire need and dependent upon the provisions of your mate in order for you to survive, you diminish yourself in her eyes. Even if your insides scream out that that is true, it certainly is not. You may be in major *want* but you are not in *need*, so don't beg.

Needing another human being is actually an altogether false concept. You need food, air, water. You desire (maybe even strongly desire) your woman and the things she brings to your life, but you don't need her or them. When you act as if you do by begging, you're living a lie. One that will eventually make you resentful and ashamed of yourself. You're never truly free to love someone when you believe you need them. That only reduces them to an object, a substance, or a tool to meet your need.

THE BOTTOM LINE

Men at work: Ask for what you want. Ask again if need be. But by all means don't act as if your life is her responsibility.

The benefits: When you refuse to beg, you gain self-respect and you tone up your courage and discipline muscles. In addition, the Black woman you love will see your courage, discipline, and self-respect as strength. Strength is high on her list of desirable masculine attributes.

The costs: If you give up begging, you are likely to suffer the nagging question as to whether or not you missed out on something from her that you really desired, and may have gotten—if only you'd begged for it.

39. ▲ ' Rock the Boat When Necessary

To the man who loves me:
I need a strong man in my life. I need to know that you are
not afraid to bring up hard things that we'd rather ignore if
it means our relationship can be better.

—From the Black woman you love

No matter how much you and the Black woman you love have in common, how comfortably and compatibly your lives seem to connect, the fact is you are and forever shall remain two separate individuals. Individuals who were brought up in two different homes, have taste preferences, experiences, and priorities that differ either a little bit or a lot. And you are subject to see one issue in two vastly different ways.

None of this has to be a problem. Loving each other doesn't mean you have to be a perfect match in everything. In fact, if you think it does, you're likely to do anything to deny, avoid, or ignore conflict. And if you do that, your relationship will be safe, peaceful, and very superficial. Real intimacy requires that you be willing to rock the boat.

Rocking the boat involves standing up for your valid opinion even when it's contrary to hers, or sensitively but firmly challenging her inappropriate behavior even if she doesn't appreciate your doing so, or voicing your disagreement with what she may have assumed you were in agreement with, or saying no when yes would have gotten you more goodies, or bringing up that issue that the two of you hate to talk about but that you really need to.

Certainly seeing things eye-to-eye is more comfortable than having conflicting points of view, especially over something important to both of you. But because you are different, you will see, desire, and conclude differently and when you do you must be willing to say it even if it causes your love boat to drift from calm seas to choppy waters.

Fear and laziness are at the heart of a refusal to rock the boat when necessary. Fear and laziness are the enemies of love, and though they may powerfully tempt you to complacency and the comfort of unchallenged silence, they are rusty anchors that keep you and the relationship stuck in neutral and slowly sinking.

THE BOTTOM LINE

Men at work: Put away the fear-based notion that sensitive, unpleasant, or potentially volatile issues should never be brought up between the two of you. But first evaluate your timing, accuracy, communicator style, and, most important, your motives. Then where appropriate and necessary to the health of your relationship, unapologetically risk rocking the boat by raising the issue.

The benefits: If you willingly rock the boat when necessary, you and your mate will find that disagreement, conflict, and confrontation are not only honest and natural, but your effectiveness in handling them will grow with practice. Also, a significant fringe benefit is the mutual respect for each other's courage and integrity that you will gain as you sensitively, yet boldly, risk rocking the boat when needed.

The costs: Upsetting the status quo by exposing and confronting your differences is risky business. You can expect to feel at least a little unsure as to whether it's worth the risk of challenging or offending the woman you love when you'd much prefer to maintain her constant approval and admiration.

40. ■ ● ◆ *Monitor Your Complaint Output*

To the man who loves me:
To you it may be just your way of venting and getting things off your chest, but when you complain too much and it turns into this big evaluation of my performance where I grade myself, I completely turn off and make space between us. Neither way is very helpful at all.

—From the Black woman you love

You've got just as much right as your woman or anyone else to open your mouth and voice your complaints. It's not that you are demanding perfection of your mate and your relationship or any other part of your life, right? It's just that if things could be better than things already are how can they get better if you don't say something. There's nothing wrong with your noticing what you'd like to see changed, improved upon, or terminated, or even your having a serious beef about it, but there could be something terribly wrong and ultimately destructive with voicing your every complaint every time.

A major component of your woman's self-image and her passion in life is derived from feeling approved of and wonderfully acceptable to you, the man who loves her. She thrives on knowing you have not only accepted what you can see of her with your naked eye, but that you have looked beneath the surface into her private interior where her motives and intentions, her tastes, opinions, values, and character—her true self—reside. And she wants to be sure that even there you find her not only acceptable, but impressive. Your opinion of her matters more than anyone else's besides her own (in fact, to some women your opinion matters far more than it should).

When there is an all too steady flow of complaints and criticism from you (especially when there is not at least twice as much praise), she begins to believe that you see her as damaged goods. When that happens for too long her capacity to love you and receive love from you as well as her courage to respond to even your valid complaints diminishes. Intimate relationship with you becomes to her a dangerous place where your disapproval and her shame threaten to overwhelm her.

Even if all your complaints aren't directed at her, the nurturing, care-giving tendency in women sometimes crosses the line into feeling responsible somehow to make all your complaints go away. Women are prone to internalizing blame that's not theirs and that you never meant for them to have in the first place.

THE BOTTOM LINE

Men at work: You can forever wonder why she is the way she is and why you need to monitor your complaint output, or you can, at great sacrifice, sensitively and wisely keep your lesser complaints to yourself. If your complaint is merely motivated by a desire to let off some steam, moan and groan over a pet peeve, or enforce your nitpicky standards, swallow it.

The benefits: Monitoring your complaint output keeps the air cleaner between you two and it makes the complaints you do raise get taken more seriously, because you won't be considered a man who gripes all the time.

The costs: Having to figure which complaints are acceptable and which aren't, and allowing to stand uncorrected some minor beefs about her or your relationship.

41. ■ ● ◆ *Adjust Your Tone of Voice*

To the man who loves me:
When you raise your voice at me, I shut down. Then it's hard for me to even care what you're talking about. I don't want to shut down, but I don't want you to manhandle me with your mouth, either.

—From the Black woman you love

To a woman everything means something. Obviously *what* you say communicates to her, but *how* you say it does too. As a matter of fact, your tone of voice can make all the difference as to whether your words are truly heard. The volume, inflection, and the general attitude behind your words always say something—be it positive or negative—about her and about your relationship.

She can't help but be attuned to how you speak to her, whether it's full of hard edges and loud noises or steady restraint and well-modulated tones. You may need to adjust your levels to get away from the former and closer to the latter.

Don't forget she is descended from foremothers who were uprooted and brought to a land where they were verbally abused and commonly addressed as "Gal," "Mammy," or "Auntie." Later, they were made to feel shame for staying home to tend to babies and keep house and badgered into the workplace. Once they got there they were loudly criticized for doing so well and thus "undermining their man's ability to succeed." Even now, no matter how great their efforts and their contributions, they too often have to endure some fool somewhere disrespecting her or her sisters with boisterous demands, ridicule, or offensive labels.

If you fail, even infrequently, to keep a sensitive, respectful tone of voice with her, it can have a devastating effect on her ability to trust that, when all's said and done, you mean her well.

You see, every time you open your mouth to say anything to her, she has to gear up for what could be a tone that blesses or one that curses her. Believe me, it matters to her which one it is. By adjusting your tone you have the power to decide.

THE BOTTOM LINE

Men at work: Never raise your voice to a point that offends or frightens her (her eyes will confirm it for you). Avoid stinging sarcasm and condescending remarks intended to set her straight. Wait until you have complete control over your anger before you discuss volatile matters with her. Temporarily interrupt the conversation if your tone gets salty. Don't make excuses or apologies for your anger or hurt feelings. Always apologize for the inappropriate attitude or actions that result from it.

The benefits: Keeping an agreeable and appropriate tone of voice when speaking to her can help undo some of the destructive effects of the verbal disrespect your woman may have experienced from others. You'll show yourself to be a man of respect and self-control. She will not only admire and appreciate you for that, she will feel secure and esteemed in your presence.

The costs: You may feel restricted and a little less spontaneous by the need to monitor your mouth.

42. Share Her Load

To the man who loves me:
Help . . . !

—From the Black woman you love

Everything about loving a Black woman is not centered in passionate feelings, romantic gestures, and sensitively speaking each other's language of love. As important as all those may be, if your love for her doesn't express itself in mundane, practical, day-to-day affairs of life, your love is too high in the clouds. It needs to be brought back down to earth.

There's nothing more intimate or loving than choosing to bear or share some of the responsibilities and obligations that make her days full and her nights weary. Wherever you can, as much as you can, share in or take over some of the demanding tasks on her personal to-do list. Especially those that benefit you as well.

The worst thing you can do is to get hung up on non-issues like "that's woman's work." If you buy into that foolishness, you could easily end up with a woman who's doing a "man's job" eight hours a day, earning a "man's check," and then coming home to another shift doing "woman's work"—not fair. By all means, share her load.

Though many women seem to be handling it well, keeping the pace and balancing all their demanding responsibilities, they are too often sacrificing adequate self-care, rest, and recreation in order to keep up. In the short term they look like highly efficient, ultra-organized superwomen. In the long term, much to their men's disappointment, they often because exhausted, resentful, passionless souls who just want to be left alone.

No question about it, you are certain to be quite busy yourself, and to do what I'm suggesting may mean some of the items on your to-do list may get delayed or completely erased. In a word, I'm talking about sacrifice and by definition that means it will cost you. Do it anyway. Help lighten her load. Lower some of your expectations and requirements of her and, by all means, decrease the frequency of your requests and complaints. Let her see that your love for her is willing to show up and help out where she may least expect it.

THE BOTTOM LINE

Men at work: Permanently, if you can, or temporarily if you can't, assume some of the work in your relationship that has been exclusively, or mostly, hers. For example, do some shopping sometimes, or cook, or find the baby-sitter, or clean the house, or make the travel arrangements, or keep the appointment . . . Don't require that she lavish praise or gratitude on you. Just take on the tasks willingly and regularly.

The benefits: As you work to share her load, you will learn firsthand the rigorous demands on her life, which will stir you to new levels of respect and appreciation for her. She will feel tremendously supported by your efforts and your selfless attitude. She will develop new levels of respect and appreciation for you. The result—mutually satisfying love.

The costs: The expenditure of your already heavily extended time and energy. You may also resent the possibility that if you share her load she'll see it only as your doing what you should have been doing in the first place rather than a special act of love worthy of some form of recognition.

43. *Let Her Help You*

To the man who loves me:
You'd probably be surprised by how much I do that truly
benefits so many other people in my life. I still don't know
what would be wrong with your being one of those people.

—From the Black woman you love

Unlike men, who measure real strength by how much they can accomplish on their own, women are more apt to measure it by how much they can get done together. The Black woman you have has or once had and can recover a sincere desire to share in the responsibilities that grab your attention, consume your time, and stimulate your abilities. She wants to help you do what you do because helping you is one vital way she experiences herself as a part of you.

In minor matters like balancing your checkbook or unpacking your luggage or reminding you of your appointments or organizing your closet, and in major ones like getting your new business up and running or working out your IRS problem or settling a breach between you and your children, if she loves you, her two goals are:

1. To help your life work easier and better.
2. To merge with you in the intimacy of making another "you alone" activity become an "us together" one.

Though that may be her intention, to you it can feel like she's hovering over you, doubting your ability, interrupting, interfering, and trying to take control. All of which are complete turnoffs for you. Granted there are some Black women who *are* doing just that and it understandably makes you want to keep your business to yourself. But they are not the norm. More likely the woman in your life yearns to experience the joy of offering her help to you and knowing you'll accept and value it.

You know firsthand how satisfying that can be, because men love to give assistance to their women. They just feel funny when women try to return the favor. Now is the time to change the lopsided arrangement. You can be sure you need to change if:

• Your most common response to her offer to help you is "That's all right I've got it covered," or
• You say yes to her help, then take the task back over that she was performing for you, or
• You try to keep your most challenging responsibilities a secret from her, or

- You can't fully enjoy your accomplishments if she gave you a helping hand, or
- Your woman never offers to help you anymore.

THE BOTTOM LINE

Men at work: Because to your woman it's not just a job that needs to be done, it's the opportunity to share love with her man by being active in the things that make up your life, look for ways to include her and solicit her help. Or sometimes take her up on her offer to assist you. You'll miss out on what she can offer if you only show appreciation for her abilities, instead of making comments about how you love working together.

The benefits: Practically speaking, you'll get help to get done what's important to you, which will make it possible for you to be even more productive and efficient. But even more importantly, your woman will get the vital emotional benefits of being welcomed into your private world of responsibilities. Your willingness to depend on her is yet another indication of the bond of closeness that exists between the two of you. It's what she thrives on.

The costs: It may be hard for you to appreciate your own accomplishments when you know you had help. Also, it could take some extra time and effort to show her what you're trying to do and how she can and cannot be of assistance. You also run the risk that she'll add her touches and the results won't end up exactly the way they would have if you did the whole thing yourself.

44. ▲ ■ ● ◆ ▶ *Resist Procrastination*

To the man who loves me:
Sometimes I just watch you, you get so busy planning and preparing yourself to go for it, then when it's time to make a move—any move—you start planning and preparing all over again. That's when I want to ask so badly, "Baby what are you waiting for?"

—From the Black woman you love

The good news is women are beginning to more fully understand and appreciate that a man's love is often expressed by what he does and what he doesn't do, rather than by nouns, verbs, and adjectives. So your actions have become vital to her trust in your love. The bad news is when you don't quite get around to the doing of things, your love begins to smell like a fake. Procrastination is recognizing the need, desire, and opportunity to meet a goal, having a strategy to accomplish the goal, rallying your resources—and then delaying on the follow-through.

When men fail to follow through, especially when they habitually fail to follow through, their women stop trusting them. When they can't trust you, their sense of security diminishes, and when their sense of security dies their love for you has lost its foundation. It's especially important in loving a Black woman that you not commit to action and make promises that you are not willing come hell or high water to act on. It's okay to dream, to contemplate, and to consider out loud, but when you do, call it that. To imply that it's something you *will* do and then you don't is not taken lightly or easily dismissed by the woman you love even if it feels like no big thing to you.

Fear of failure (which often only means fear of missing perfection) is at the root of procrastination. It can keep you meaning to act but waiting endlessly for the "right" conditions (i.e., the advance guarantee that all will go perfectly). The pain of past letdowns, failures, and disappointing performances can often tempt us to hesitate on follow-through. Nobody wants to rerun a failure, so we tend to avoid the situations where we've already experienced some failure. But for your sake and hers, you must try again. No one succeeds who's not willing to fail.

So go ahead and pay the bill, make the appointment, keep the promise, fix the thing, clean up the misunderstanding, make the apology, return the call, do the job, sign up, pay up, show up, or speak up. Throw off your procrastination and follow through.

THE BOTTOM LINE

Men at work: Identify three to five things you need to do and have been procrastinating on. Put them in order from the most to least challenging. Share your list with the woman in your life (only if yours is a fairly significant relationship) and your time line to follow through (sooner beats later hands down). Start with the least challenging, do it, and move on to the next. Note: Don't require that your mate be thrilled and impressed in order for you to be motivated to continue to follow through.

The benefits: You get things done that are important to you and the woman you love. Also, acting, instead of avoiding, will help you to shake off the vague, shadowy fears that bind you to inactivity. You'll also help foster a sense of security in your woman, which ignites her respect for you, which in turn enhances your self-respect.

The costs: To resist procrastination is to choose to walk into the anxiety-inducing unknown, where you can't be 100 percent sure of the outcome and where you're likely to be confronted with your own faults, fears, and self-doubts.

45. ▲ ■ ● ◆ *Be Patient*

To the man who loves me:
I have found out again and again that if I wait for you it
will usually be well worth the wait. I guarantee you it works
the other way around too. Give me the time I need and
you'll be glad you did.

—From the Black woman you love

When you merge men's concrete, goal-oriented style and women's more intuitive, feelings-oriented style in a balanced, well-integrated way, it's amazing how much the two of you can accomplish together. Your two strengths are halves of a highly efficient, mutually benefiting whole. Each approach, though, has its pluses and minuses, the bitter and the sweet. To get all the good of your woman's style, you'll need to put up with what you'll see as the drawbacks. You'll need to exercise patience or end up missing out on the vital positive contributions that emerge from your woman's natural style.

Abstract-thinking "feelers" can be slower to take action than concrete-thinking "doers," just as concrete-thinking doers can be slower to know and share feelings. In a multitude of ways the Black woman you love will, by her internally driven approach as compared to your externally driven one, seem to be slower than you'd like her to be when it comes to deciding, strategizing, and acting. When you want hard answers and competent choices, she may still be firmly planted at the think-it-through, feel-it-out-and-talk-it-over stage, getting a handle on what's happening inside herself about the issue. All the while you're ready to do what it takes to get the matter quickly crossed off your list so you can move on to the next item.

But when you rush her, requiring that she merely consider the cold hard facts alone in order to make a move, you stifle what's natural to her and demand she act like you—and that she be quick about it! Just like you may need loads of extra time to process internal stuff like definitive answers, final choices, and her course of action, she won't necessarily be ready to give you her bottom line just because you're ready to hear it.

Be patient with her. She needs time to analyze the matter and what to say or do about it by breaking it all down to at least three parts: the emotional, the intellectual, and the intuitive. Then she'll need to put them all back together again before she can wholeheartedly commit to action. The weightier the question, decision, or behavior, the more time she may need to be able to make a move.

Your standing over her tapping your toes nervously on the floor or making any attempts to coerce her to a "facts only" conclusion will just frustrate her and come across as insensitive and unsupportive. All of which will at the very least slow down her processing time, and perhaps even shut down the entire process altogether.

THE BOTTOM LINE

Men at work: When you need her input, choices, answers, or commitment to action in a matter that's important to the two of you, approach her not just with the facts but with your feelings and the process by which you arrived at your choice as to what to do. Patiently entertain her questions and allow her to think out loud without using pushy, hard-sell tactics. Ask her, "At what time or on what day will you be ready to give me a bottom-line answer on this? And how can I help you get one?" If, at that moment, she delays giving a conclusive response, then repeat the process with a good attitude as many times as is necessary.

The benefits: She'll bring to the table the strength of her thoughtful, intuitive nature, which can be beneficial when added to your "just get it done" approach. By being patient you give her space to do it her way—in spite of how different her way is from yours. Your woman sees that as truly loving sensitivity and respect for her.

The costs: All the extra time that you'd rather not have to invest in just trying to get some answers or in action.

46. ▲ ◆ *Keep Your Fascination with Passing Women to Yourself*

To the man who loves me:
Please, don't accuse me of being insecure or jealous when I
say this. Being out with you anywhere makes me feel proud.
Proud that we hold such love, respect, and desire for each
other. But when you gaze so long and hard at some other
woman, it seems like a piece of your love, respect, and desire
for me has been loaned out to her.

—From the Black woman you love

It can happen anytime. Even when it's the last thing on your mind and you're in the last place you'd ever expect it to. As if out of nowhere she enters your field of vision—on the elevator, at the mall, on TV, at a stoplight, or even in church on Sundays, just as you open your eyes from praying. She's one of the dozens of eye-catching and worthy-of-a-second-look beauties who innocently cross your path daily, and whom you innocently (at least at first) can't help but notice.

A few of them *are* drop-dead gorgeous and everyone in the place stops what they're doing for just a second or two to pay tribute to her. More often, though, she is not the type you'd find on any magazine cover, but she does have some attention-arresting quality, like a fabulous physique, or thoroughly hooked-up attire, or a sharp "do," visible poise and confidence, a multimillion-dollar smile, or she plain drips with some indefinable, highly charged sexual energy. Whatever it is, when she passes, you notice her, and for a moment, your eyes linger and that mechanism inside your neck makes your head swivel to follow her, as your jaw drops open and a barely (or loudly) audible "umm, oomph, oomph, oopmh!" sounds forth from your mouth before you can stop it. (We won't even go into the sweaty palms, the racing heart, and elevated blood pressure that afflicts some men at these times.)

When all this occurs it means that, for a second or two, you were fascinated by the visuals—and *usually* that's all it means. That brief moment blows over and your life goes on.

But when you are in the company of the Black woman you love, and your eyes wander, at the very least it is likely to annoy her, or it could possibly wound her deeply. To her, even the little bit of time you invested in following your fascination was time and attention you gave to a woman who was not your woman. Though you may have no intention of letting anything else wander but your eye, you will have "innocently" given away what your woman wants most from you.

That means, if you're not careful, several times a day you could, in an instant, chip away at your woman's trust, security, and the respect for her feelings that to her define love. Your best bet is to keep your fascination with passing women discreetly to yourself. Because the truth is, looks *can* kill.

THE BOTTOM LINE

Men at work: If your admiring looks are in fact brief and harmless (i.e., not flirting or fixating), practice making them even briefer by downscaling to an imperceptible side-glance as she passes. Restrain all your "fascinated" body language and sound effects. Better yet, let her come to your eyes rather than your eyes going to her.

The benefits: If you discipline your eyes and keep your fascinated moments few, you'll save yourself a lot of grief. Most men don't mind big arguments over what they see as big issues. But you'll get frustrated in a hurry by how big a fight can arise just because of one lingering look.

The costs: You may resent this advice—and the Black woman who wants you to follow it—because it'll seem to you that she's being way too needy, insecure, and demanding. And you might feel deprived, like you're missing out on something important.

47. ■ ● ◆ ◗ *Hold Her Even When You Don't Have To*

To the man who loves me:
When you hold me I can figure out so much. I can tell if everything is all right with us or if there's something we need to clean up. I can tell if there's anything weighing on you heavily of if you are excited or if you're content. What thrills me most is knowing that you'll reach out for me and hold me tight regardless of the state of your feelings or our circumstances.

—From the Black woman you love

Most men have learned to live with the fact that the women in their lives generally can appreciate being held or embraced nearly any time. The feel of your physical presence wrapped, joined, clasped, bound, or otherwise connected to hers is one of her most treasured natural experiences. There are few, and for some women no, circumstances under which she would not delight in simply being held close by you.

Many Black women, maybe even yours, would love to get far more holding than their men give. And even though they have learned to live without it and seldom make requests for it anymore, they yearn for it deeply.

Often men feel as if they have their hands full with what should, ought, and must be done, in the million and one parts of their fast-moving lives. It's easy to only think to hold her when you "have to," like when she outright says hold me and you suspect it will cost you if you don't, or those times when you feel as if you should say *something*, but you don't know what to say so you have to hold her.

But holding the Black woman you love only when you must makes you merely a reactor to her spoken or implied requests, or to your own crisis-averting instincts. Reactors don't initiate, they just respond.

Actors (not in the phony role-playing, but action-initiating sense) take steps, not just to avoid or remedy a problem, but to give a good thing because it's a good thing and they have all the power it takes to give it freely.

THE BOTTOM LINE

Men at work: To her, deeply satisfying love is made up of the frequent intimate, caring "micro-moments," rather than every now and then major events. When she least expects it, tell her, "I'd love to just hold you close for a moment, is that all right with you." Practice telling her briefly why you choose to hold her.

The benefits: When you hold her without being asked or made to she feels cherished and is freshly and powerfully reminded of your delight in her. It communicates intimacy, acceptance, and commitment. It will appeal to you because it is a thoroughly uncomplicated way for you to express a whole lot of your love in a little bit of your time. And you're not likely to ever be chided for doing it too much. There's virtually no such thing as "excessive holding."

The costs: Don't hold or caress or any of those nonverbals instead of talking out an issue between the two of you. Your holding can become too mechanical and automatic if you're not careful.

48. ■ ● ◆ *Surprise Her*

To the man who loves me:
For you to be a man who's stable, dependable, and consistent means a lot to me. But it sure doesn't mean that you shouldn't feel free to shake things up a little. I trust you. Feel free to surprise me sometimes.

—From the Black woman you love

One of the richest things about love is the fact that when it is at its best you are willing to offer your partner what is highly treasured by her, *because* it's treasured by her. Even though it may be something that means very little to you.

Most men learned a long time ago that most women love surprises offered for love's sake. It's a good bet that the Black woman in your life is included in that number. It's also a pretty good bet that surprises don't mean anywhere near as much to you. Being caught off guard and the suspicion that you will be required to spontaneously show some big, loud, shocked, pleased, and appreciative emotion is probably not your idea of a good time.

But to her the totally unexpected, caring, usually unrequested presentation of something from your creative mind, or your generous heart, or your caring hand, ranks among her greatest joys. It's not even about how much it cost or how impressed anybody else might be with the surprise, it's that you, with all the things you could have done with your time, energy, and resources, considered her and brought some joy to her life. Above all she's utterly taken by the obvious fact that you did it just because you wanted to. As often as you can, surprise her.

You needn't wait for the "expected surprises," occasions like birthdays, holidays, and anniversaries. Whenever and as often as you decide to is the right time:

- Surprise her by doing something for her that she expected to have to do herself (fill her gas tank, run her errands, cook her dinner).
- Surprise her by calling, writing, faxing, or e-mailing a one-liner like "I am so unbelievably blessed that I woke up this morning with you in my life."
- Surprise her with a fresh rose on her pillow or a bouquet sent to her at work.
- Surprise her by doing something *her* way for a change.
- Surprise her by sharing some of your deepest thoughts and hidden feelings without being asked to.
- Surprise her by showing up exactly when you promised and not a minute later.
- Surprise her by giving her two surprises in one day.

THE BOTTOM LINE

Men at work: Keep your creative juices flowing (and any tendencies toward self-centeredness in check) by blessing the Black woman you love with frequent and varied surprises. At the bare minimum, never let a week pass without making at least one happen.

The benefits: Beyond all the appreciative laughter, her delight at being caught off guard, and her anticipation of just what you might come up with next is the powerfully affirming fact that you went out of your way for her. In that glorious moment you caused your sweet, creative surprise to come out of nowhere and land in her life. By doing so you simultaneously hoisted her up on a pedestal, and reminded her, once again, that she is a precious treasure to you.

The costs: The risk that she'll turn the tables on you and expect you to show the same level of enthusiasm and appreciation as she did, or you'll have hurt feelings to deal with.

49. ▲◗ *Let Her Romance You*

To the man who loves me:
I would love to see you sit back and relax and let me show
you the kind of romantic evening that you'd never forget.
One of these days I guess I'll be able to once I figure out how
to keep you from beating me to the punch.

—From the Black woman you love

If given half a chance, Black women are perfectly capable of romancing the men who love them. In fact, they are not only capable, many of them have no shortage of the creativity and the desire to express themselves romantically. Be assured you are not solely responsible for designing and financing all the dates, coming up with all the surprises, or initiating all the imaginative displays of affection. She can do it too and she will if you let her. Somewhere along the way men and women made an unspoken agreement that men must be the romancers and women must be the romanced. Many men got really good at the job, and their women were altogether thrilled by it. But always, when a really good thing only travels on a one-way street, somebody ends up overworked and somebody else ends up lazy. Romance needs to travel both directions.

Many women have come to believe that only men can be the pursuers, so they sit and wait, and sit and wait some more for men to notice and pursue them. These women are convinced that it is somehow "unladylike" for her to approach an attractive, desirable man. Obviously there are some right ways and some ridiculous ways to do it but both of you should do it.

Often men who love Black women suspect that if she expects you to arrange all the sweet romancing and you don't do it then you'll be brought up on charges and convicted of gross negligence. Liberate yourself and your woman. Declare it's a new day where all is fair in love. You may be surprised to discover that she'd love to ask for your number, or take you out to dinner, or send you flowers, or tickets to the game, or a romantic CD or . . .

You'll also discover that there is no shame in the game for you to absolutely love it when she romances you too.

THE BOTTOM LINE

Men at work: Say yes to her attempts to romance you. Give up responding with anything like "Baby, you don't have to do that"; instead focus on encouraging her to be creative. Enjoy yourself thoroughly and applaud her romantic efforts lavishly.

The benefits: You get to relax more and experience the deep satisfaction that comes from seeing how much the Black woman in your life truly desires you, as evidenced by the way she puts her feelings into action. She gets the benefit of being freed to develop and express her romance repertoire.

The costs: If you let her take some of the romantic responsibilities you will have to share the credit and the applause for those fabulously romantic goings-on. Also, if all you two do is completely flip from you do it all, to she does it all, you will still be out of balance and no better off than before.

50. ▲ ■ ● ◆ ◗ *Tell the Truth*

To the man who loves me:
I know what it's like to be lied to . . . little white lies as well as huge completely uncalled for ones that take me by total surprise. The fact is, our relationship can't ever be the real thing if we don't give each other the truth. I make that commitment to you. Please, give me that in return.

—From the Black woman you love

Your life is probably much more complicated already than you would like it to be. The simple day-to-day things that you have to deal with to keep your world moving forward and not sliding backward already take up more of your thought, energy, and effort than you'd prefer. So when it comes to relating effectively to the Black woman in your life, the way to keep complications to a minimum is to simply tell the truth. Always. Period. When it's convenient and when it's not. She doesn't need to know everything on your mind or every detail of your existence, but whatever you do share for her sake and yours let it be the bold-faced 100 percent, genuine truth. Telling her the truth won't always get you applause, admiration, and appreciation. In fact, sometimes the truth will cause her pain, sadness, or anger, because the truth may be disappointingly different from what she wanted to believe about you and about the two of you together.

But when you lie, you're using words to offer the woman you love a counterfeit version of reality. It may make her smile, calm her fears, and temporarily increase your approval rating, but ultimately when you're found out it will destroy what matters even more to her, and that is her trust in you. No matter how much you gain in the short term by not telling the truth, in the long term lying to her insults her, and creates distance between the two of you.

Lies, exaggerations, creative deceptions, false promises, denials, and conveniently left out facts and figures can be tempting to use from time to time. They can handily pull us out of a jam or put us into a sweeter situation. You're probably not trying to hurt her with a mistruth. More likely you're shrinking or stretching the truth to keep her from getting hurt. But no hurt you save her from by deception is as devastating as the pain of discovering that you were willing to let her live with a lie in the first place. She'll feel foolish because she'll know that, for whatever reason, you "played" her. And she fell for it.

Even if they were little white lies about what you consider lightweight issues, you could end up doing heavyweight damage. Because when you play fast and loose with the truth, you have an unfair advantage over her that makes her vulnerable. Her survival instincts warn her that if you're a lover who'll lie, you have the power to devastate her life—before she'd even know what hit her! That's too dangerous a position for many women to tolerate. They'll want to flee to safety before little lies become giant ones that could cause her major losses.

THE BOTTOM LINE

Men at work: Even when it won't put you in a more favorable light or guarantee your most desired outcome, commit to telling the truth and nothing but the truth.

The benefits: When you tell the truth, she gets an accurate picture of who you are and how you operate. She finds security in the knowledge that though you are not perfect, you are honest, and your honesty demands honesty in return. Also, by telling the truth you never have to go through all the complicated changes of adding more lies to keep the original one in place.

The costs: The truth may hurt. You run the risk that what you honestly report could disappoint her or disgrace you. Telling the truth is always the most moral choice, but not necessarily the most comfortable one.

51. ●◆◗ *Explain*

To the man who loves me:
I am ready to care, to listen, to understand, and maybe even
to agree. But that won't matter much if you won't tell me not
only where you're coming from but how you got there.

—From the Black woman you love

Black women and the men who love them seem to come from two different planets when it comes to their communication styles. Men are naturally focused on how the story ends. Getting to the point quickly is what's most important to you, not messing around with the boring details. Women do just the opposite.

Communication is not about right ways or wrong ways. It's about effective ones or ineffective ones. Whatever works, works. With a Black woman explaining the details, not just announcing the bottom line, works.

Everyone wants to be heard and not just heard but understood. Women hear and understand you best when you take the time to explain the step-by-step and blow-by-blow details of how you arrived at your bottom line. Unless you explain the whys and wherefores, the thoughts, circumstances, feelings, and motivations that shaped your ultimate decision, perspective, or remark, women are likely to 1) feel barred from entry to the most vital and appealing part of you—your thoughts and feelings; welcome access there is what intimacy is all about to her; 2) assume you really didn't put any thought into making the decision or drawing the conclusion, which could lead her to have little respect for your approach to thinking through issues. Unless you clue her in, when you unveil your bottom line but give no details, they'll never know you may have been carefully processing the details for days before you even uttered a word.

When you leave out the details and tell her only your point, for example: "I've decided we should take a break from each other for a while." Or, "Would you be my wife?" Or, "On the first of the month I'm quitting my job," you can expect to see that dazed, confused, hungry look on her face that says, "Hold on . . . Wait just a minute. Would you please back up from Z and explain the details from A, B, and C to me?"

Women are notoriously process-oriented. They enjoy sharing with each other all the rich details of matters that concern them. Don't assume that they lack the ability to reason objectively, draw logical conclusions, and make concrete decisions. Yes, they are "thinkers" too, and not "feelers" only.

But the more intuitive side of them traffics in details. The more vivid and comprehensive the details, the greater their ability to grasp and respond to the issue. The work of probing, clarifying, and analyzing details is so important to them that they may go overboard sharing the process with you, and making you have to wait to interrupt to ask for the bottom line. They may expect you to be the way they are and misinterpret what it means that you aren't.

Men are notoriously performance-oriented. If you must, you'll tolerate the annoying details and seemingly inconsequential nature of a matter just long enough to figure out what to do about it. You're looking for the all-important bottom line. To you, this is the streamlined, efficient approach. And you're more than willing, at the end, to share with your woman what you came up with. But if you really want her to hear, understand, and respect your bottom line, you definitely need to give her the details along with it. You needn't feel you must defend your position, but you should explain it.

THE BOTTOM LINE

Men at work: The more important the issue, decision, suggestion, or problem, when you share your bottom line with her, take the time to summarize what led you to it. Be willing to respond to her many questions about it, knowing she is probably not trying to shoot holes in your conclusion, but is only expressing her process-oriented, details-seeking style.

The benefits: When you give the details along with your bottom line you open the door for her to your private world of thoughts, feelings, and motivations. All of which communicate a special kind of naked trust and intimacy to her. Also, it's the only way to make sure that she has accurately understood your point as you meant it, rather than as she interpreted it after she filled in the blank spots you left.

The costs: It will feel so inefficient, time-consuming, and intrusive to have to articulate details to her that hold little value or interest to you now that you know what you plan to do.

52. ▲ ■ ● ◆ ◗
Keep Her Secrets

To the man who loves me:
I deliberately take the risk of sharing with you what I kept
secret from others. I love the idea of your wanting to know
me fully and that you won't take those deeply private parts of
who I am and carelessly display them for the world to see.

—From the Black woman you love

Her secrets are your woman's most private possessions. She carries them in a safely guarded place inside her where absolutely no one has entry—except that rare companion to whom she grants it. Once she begins to trust that yours is a love with some weight and substance to it, she'll want to share her secrets with you. She longs to be open, vulnerable, naked and not ashamed, because she can have faith in your integrity.

No matter what you hear, what you think, or how you feel about it, what's crucial here is keeping her secrets as if they were your own. Though there should be room for some failings in any truly loving relationship, I assure you, keeping her secrets is the last place you should ever be caught failing.

Her deepest, most fiercely protected secrets are probably not very different in nature from the kind you have. They have to do with the various twists, turns, and detours of her life. The private thoughts behind her public image. Her fears as well as her faults. Her hopes and yearnings. Her freshest scars and her oldest regrets. The things that cause her to laugh or weep even when no one sees her do either of them. Though some of her secrets may shock or offend you, most will only add detail, definition, and vivid color to your image of the Black woman you love. Knowing her insides will help you discover the target places to apply your love.

For women, open, vulnerable self-disclosure is an essential ingredient for building intimacy. As risky as it is for her to unwrap, unveil, and uncover her business to you (especially to you), the idea of being able to is tremendously appealing to her. It's not that she delights in danger for danger's sake, it's that making herself vulnerable to the threatening possibility that you could use the secrets she volunteers to destroy or dismiss her is far outweighed by the deeply rewarding possibility that you will handle her secrets with the utmost care.

When you do, you honor her with the kind of acceptance and support that confirms to her that, even in the shadow of her secrets, she is not alone.

THE BOTTOM LINE

Men at work: When it comes to hearing her secrets, be receptive and nonjudgmental and permanently closed-mouthed about them. Never let them slip out to others for the sake of building a case for yourself or telling a juicy story. Never throw her secrets up in her face again as payback or punishment.

The benefits: Knowing and keeping her secrets is by far one of the most meaningful ways that you could ever confirm and demonstrate your love for her. They provide you the opportunity to do what is naturally and deeply satisfying to men, protecting the women they love.

The costs: To know her secrets and refuse to criticize, publicize, or criminalize them means you lose out on being able to use them when you need ammunition in a conflict with her. Also, you'll never get to conveniently use her secrets as a way to explain or excuse your own failures in the relationship.

53. ■ ● ◆ ❭ *Resist the Urge to Punish Her*

To the man who loves me:
When you are angry with me, your punishing ways really
sting. I feel as if I have been left alone out in the cold. Pay-
back doesn't become you. I can actually feel it suffocate my
love for you.

—From the Black woman you love

If your relationship with a Black woman has any depth to it, and even a brief history, you can count on the fact that she will at some point make you angry. In fact, if she's the woman you love she'll probably make you more angry than anyone else can. When she does—as your jaws grow tight and your collar gets hot—please be sure not to give into the temptation to punish, scold, or condemn her. Do deal with the issue. Let her know that she has royally ticked you off when she has. But get a grip on yourself, or the urge to punish and pay back could get the best of you.

There's no other person with whom you have so fully invested yourself and exposed your insides than the woman you love. That means there's no one who better knows where your buttons are—and how to push them—than she does. When fears or frustrations overtake her, she may express it by giving you major mouth or what you consider an all-too-salty attitude. She may start making a valid point, but in the escalation of emotions and volume levels, your response or lack of response may lead her to step over the line and say or do something that thoroughly works your nerves.

Punishing paybacks include withholding affection, threats of retaliation, harsh verbal attacks, sabotaging or shaming her, and general meanness. Punishment is focused on revenge and one-upmanship. Neither of which has any place at all in your relationship.

As justified as you may believe yourself to be, it is never okay to use your power (whether verbal, physical, psychological, or otherwise) to punish her for her "sin." No matter how tough she talks, the fact is, you have the power to humiliate her. When you are angry, hurt, or embarrassed, you could be tempted to do just that, with the intimidating punishment of a big bully or the cold, detached, indifferent payback that silently yet forcefully declares "as far as I'm concerned you no longer exist." Don't give in to it.

THE BOTTOM LINE

Men at work: Don't let her, anyone, or anything else become your justification for punishing. Talk together about what she's said or done that ticked you off. Take the risk of telling her not just how wrong it was, but exactly how you were hurt by it. Don't insist that she endorse your every accusation and offer herself up for your rebukes and chastisements.

The benefits: By refusing to give in to the urge to punish your woman when she has angered you, you powerfully demonstrate the kind of love you have for her. It's a love that exercises self-control and offers her a tender yet truthful response even when provoked, disappointed, or enraged.

The costs: You'll sacrifice the short-term satisfaction that getting angry and getting even provide when you feel you've been wronged.

54. ■● *Season Your Criticism with Praise*

To the man who loves me:
I have never pretended to be perfect. You have helped open
my eyes to some things about myself and how I handle
things that I could stand to improve. I appreciate that you
are so direct and honest. But maybe you could sometimes
also tell me directly and honestly what I'm doing right.

—From the Black woman who loves you

Have you ever experienced times when your comments, criticisms, or complaints directed at the Black woman you love ended up packing far more force than you intended? You certainly did intend to make a point. A point you considered quite valid. A constructive criticism about the way she did or didn't handle something. What you did *not* intend was for your point to wound the woman you love. But by the look in her eyes and the droop of her shoulders and the tone of her voice you realized that your criticism did more tearing down than building up.

To women, words tend to have more nuances, secondary meanings, and implications than with men. Women rely heavily on words to convey meaning when they speak to each other. There are complex levels of meaning behind their phrasing, intonation, and choice of words. When they speak, they are not just trying to deliver news but they are very attuned to the effect on their listener of the emotional and relational dynamics behind the words.

Men, on the other hand, tend to use words to perform more basic and direct functions. You are bottom-line-oriented and pick words, tone, and body language for the simple functional purpose of making your point about the issue at hand.

These differences between men and women have led to men viewing women's communication style as too wordy, indirect, and vague. And women finding men too blunt, insensitive, and thoughtless.

When it comes to voicing a criticism to the woman you love, your best bet is to add some sincere words of praise, commendation, and encouragement. Otherwise, your criticism, as legitimate and constructive as it may be, could be met by her defensiveness or angry dismissal of you, your criticism, and your motives. Your approval and acceptance mean the world to her. When you pour on the criticism and leave out the praise, it makes it too easy for her to feel cast out from the place of your approval.

For example, don't just say, "You've overdrawn the account again. I wish you'd pay closer attention to the balance before you write a check." Add to it something like "And I really appreciate how you've been making sure lately that all our bills have been paid on time."

Don't just say, "I've told you, I don't care for surprise parties. I wish you hadn't done this behind my back." Add to it, "I am amazed at all the work and trouble you went through for my birthday."

Your words of praise go a long way in helping your words of criticism be heard and given the consideration they deserve.

THE BOTTOM LINE

Men at work: Go overboard for a while adding a B part (praise) to your A part (criticism) with the woman you love. Keep at it until the awkward, inauthentic feelings in you subside, and the injured, discarded feelings in her subside.

The benefits: She'll begin to trust that your criticism doesn't mean condemnation and cruel rejection. It just means you have a negative but necessary concern that needn't threaten her sense of security about your love.

The costs: When what you really want to do is throw a fit and prove a point to her about something negative, you might feel that having to add some praise will "water down" the strength of your message. You'll be worried that she'll ignore the criticism and only hear the praise.

55. ▲♪ *Don't Cheat on Her*

To the man who loves me:
How could you? . . .

—From the Black woman you love

The quickest way to inflate a man's ego and deflate a woman's trust is by your unfaithfulness. If your love for a Black woman does not offer the sincere commitment of your total faithfulness, then your love is only a pale imitation of the real thing. At the heart of an intimate, committed relationship with another person is the promise of exclusivity. It means that there are certain personal treasures (like your physical, spiritual, and emotional nakedness) that you just don't make available to any other living soul under any circumstances, because you have already pledged them to your mate. It belongs to her because you gave it to her.

Unless you are officially serving notice to the woman in your life that you are repossessing your love so that you can offer it elsewhere, be faithful to her at all costs. You do that by keeping your flirtations few, your promises sincere, and by all means keeping your zipper up. What might be the most intense pleasure of "a little harmless messing around" or the major emotional gratification of a super-secret thing on the side, your infidelity will do more damage than you can imagine to the woman you say you love and to your future together—to say nothing of the fact that being unfaithful causes your lying, cheating, and manipulating muscles to develop at a rapid pace. You could become so good at it that you are no good to any woman at all. Here, as with anything else, practice makes perfect.

Let's face it. Even if you are genuinely committed to a serious, exclusive relationship or marriage, sex is all around you. The vast numbers of available women and the comparatively small number of available men has resulted in making this a "buyer's market" for men. If it's simple, low-commitment, high adventure, part-time romance and readily available sexual opportunity that stir your hormones and weaken your will, you could repeatedly end up in big trouble. Because unless you settle the temptation issue in your own mind and heart, your groin will eventually call all the shots.

You can be sure that there will never be anything outside of you that will make you say *No!* and walk away. Fidelity, and the self-restraint it demands, comes from within. And if discipline, integrity, a rock-solid moral center, and an unshakable devotion to the woman you love aren't in you, faithfulness will be a foreign language and cheating a way of life.

Nearly any mess-up, even the most calamitous, in a relationship can be cleaned up if the two are willing to work, to change, and to forgive (not ignore, deny, or excuse, but forgive). But even one occurrence of infidelity—whether your extracurricular involvement was a way too physical thing or a way too emotional one—can destroy the very foundation of your woman's trust in you. Playing fast and loose with your already-committed affections will also cause her to experience the pain of rejection and abandonment in a way no one deserves to suffer.

Though your secret fling may have seemed trivial to you (*"It was purely a sexual thing. She didn't mean a thing to me."*) or justified (*"I know what I did was wrong. But you know you drove me to it."*), don't count on your woman believing that what you gave away was only the scraps of your passion and that she still has the best of your love.

Instead, your willingness to go behind her back will argue convincingly that she holds little value to you. Even if she is eventually willing to forgive you, how will you ever persuade her that there's no need for her to question your commitment—and your whereabouts—in the future? After your cheating has become for you a faded memory of the distant past, you are likely to look into the eyes of the Black woman you love and still see remnants of her hurt and mistrust. Her eyes, even more than her words, will constantly remind you that it really wasn't worth it to have roamed in the first place.

THE BOTTOM LINE

Men at work: If you are in, or sincerely working to build, a serious intimate relationship, avoid all high-risk people, places, and activities that you know invite the temptation to cross the faithfulness line. Enlist a male friend who knows all the gory details of your personal life and who has no problem challenging you—forcibly if need be—to get out of the path of temptation before you get in way over your head. Caution: temptation does not always come wrapped up in sexual packaging. Often it's in the innocent-looking, emotional bond developing between you and some other woman who is fast becoming your most intimate confidante/advisor, your best friend and the constant occupant of your uncensored thoughts.

The benefits: You won't need to constantly look over your shoulder, juggle your lies, or wrestle with sleep-stealing guilt about where your affections have inappropriately been deposited. Your signed, sealed, and delivered commitment to faithfulness means you'll avoid destroying the very thing that you may never be able to rebuild.

The costs: You'll deprive yourself of the thrills you could have had but chose not to.

56. ▲ ■ ● ◆ ◗ *Show Your Love by How You Handle Your Money*

To the man who loves me:
Money seems to be one of those things that gets far too much
of your attention sometimes, and at other times not enough.
I can't help but notice the way you are with your money.
Believe me, it says much to me about you.

—From the Black woman you love

Like it or not, money really does have meaning and power. Contrary to what some believe, it doesn't mean the world, and it certainly isn't *all*-powerful, but it is what you use to make happen many of the things that matter most to you and the Black woman you love. How you handle—or mishandle—it will speak volumes about you to her, much more persuasively than what you could ever say about yourself. Handling your money with care, discipline, and maturity builds a strong case that you are a caring, disciplined, and mature man. Those, of course, are the very character traits that hold the most weight to her and elicit the highest level of respect from her.

Balance is the key word when it comes to your approach to finances. If you are a man of extremes—either too cautious or too irresponsible—you'll fearfully hoard it all, or foolishly spend it all, completely obsessed with your bottom line and cash flow or totally unmoved by your zero balance and past-due bills. Either way, you spell danger to her. She'll surmise that if your relationship with money can be so out of balance, so can your relationship with her. She'll see you as not only a credit risk, but a commitment risk who makes a mess out of what most deserves to be handled with care.

Before you even jump the broom, while your money is *your* money, she doesn't get to go over your bank statements and your credit report, but she does need to know that you are both responsible and motivated enough to take care of business with consistency and balance. She will figure that out by what you actually do with your money, not what you say about it.

After vows are said and rings are swapped, your money and her money become "y'all's" money and the very currency intended to provide the financial stability of your union. Now your money-management style will directly and dramatically affect the degree of security or insecurity she will experience with you—and not just in the dollars-and-cents areas of your relationship!

THE BOTTOM LINE

Men at work: Give your spending, saving, and paying habits a brutally honest examination. Take steps to get a handle on what's out of control in your finances and within yourself. For her sake, as well as your own, begin (or continue) to operate in a responsible, consistent manner that she can count on.

The benefits: When you handle your finances sensibly, the woman in your life can breathe easier and trust you more fully. Every way in which you help to strengthen her sense of security, and decrease her anxiety and tendency toward self-protectiveness, makes her feel safe, and free to be more receptive, passionate, and affirming—the stuff you love.

The costs: To benefit from this advice may require the rigorous and often painful process of overhauling your approach to money and things. It can be traumatic, because the work must start inside you, with your attitude, discipline, and motivation. It will require courage and patience, as you're bound to unearth some excess baggage that may seem too challenging and embarrassing to face, let alone work on changing.

57. ▲ ■ ● ◆ ◗ *Become and Remain Clean and Sober*

To the man who loves me:
Because I love you I can't stand watching how you are tear-
ing up your life. And, in ways I don't think you even know,
you're tearing up mine too. I don't think I can keep on like
this with you.

—From the Black woman you love

Love is not merely an emotion, an intention, or even a commitment. These only become love when one essential ingredient is added to them—action. In other words, love is not just feeling something, it's doing something. And the kinds of somethings it takes to love another person require an amazing amount of physical, spiritual, and emotional resources.

Substance abuse is a surefire way to destroy those resources, paralyzing or short-circuiting the possibility of a mature, mutually satisfying love. The sad truth is too many Black women have been caused too many tears over too many men whose love was taken back and given over to a high. It's a tragic plague that has left both Black women and the men who love them broke, devastated, and deprived of each other's love and trust. It's the worst kind of bankruptcy.

If you're caught in the smothering quicksand of dependency on drugs, alcohol, sex, or any other out-of-control pleasure pursuits, nothing will change yesterday's broken promises and broken relationships. But today you have a fresh opportunity to take action in the name of love that surely can change the course of all your tomorrows. I urge you to get and remain clean and sober. Do it first to save your own life but also to regain the hope of being able to love without being too preoccupied to show it honestly and dependably.

The Black woman you love or loved will not be able to do it for you, nor should you expect her to continue to bear with you if you don't do it for yourself. It's likely her love won't up and leave overnight; but eventually, having you in her life will cost more than she can afford to pay. You can be sure that being with you has kept her caught up in, or headed to, a world of constant losses, bitter disappointments, and nightmarish insanity. Though she may truly wish it were not so, loving you up close is just too costly.

THE BOTTOM LINE

Men at work: Get help. Contact a counselor or a minister, or perhaps a friend who has succeeded in recovering from an addiction. Enlist their help in accessing an appropriate twelve-step program such as Alcoholics Anonymous or Cocaine Anonymous. Focus first on getting your life together, not trying to please someone else.

The benefits: You can be liberated from the bondage of your dependency. Spiritually, physically, emotionally, and relationally, you can regain your life. You can step out of your lonely, secret, and self-centered world of addiction and into the bright possibilities of mutual love and self-respect.

The costs: Admitting to yourself and to your mate that you have a problem will be hard on your sense of self-worth. Feelings of failure and discouragement and the likelihood that rigorous honesty here could cause you to lose what you value the most: your reputation and your relationship. Also, a very real fear that sobriety may be an impossible goal to attain.

58. ▲ ■ ● ◆) *Change Your Running Crowd*

To the man who loves me:
Some women swear they can tell right away if their man has
been in the company of another woman by the way he looks,
acts, and speaks afterward. I don't know about that, but I
can always tell the quality of the guys you've been hanging
out with by how you look, act, and speak when you return.

—From the Black woman you love

There are two basic varieties of running partners—the kind that are a positive influence on you and who help you rise to your highest potential in all the various areas of your life. They are your brothers, who, though imperfect, keep you grounded and remind you that a good man doesn't merely talk the talk, he must walk the walk. They are committed to walking that walk and a million different ways of helping you walk it too.

The only other kind of running partner there is, is the kind that doesn't bring anything particularly good into your life, and instead is a draining, destructive influence on you. They too come in all colors. They live everywhere from high up in the hills to down in the valley and across the tracks and everywhere in between. Even if no one else knows it, if you're honest, you know your character and your conduct go down at least a little whenever you run with them. You may hate to admit it, but they are no good for you and what you are trying to build with the Black woman in your life. Another powerful way you can add to, or subtract from, your woman's sense of security is by the poor caliber of company you keep. No, she absolutely does not have the right to dictate your list of friends, but she does see the fruit of those friendships in your life, and sometimes it's rotten to the core. Consider the following:

- If you must lie to your woman or keep secret who you are spending time with, you need to change your running crowd.
- If your friends disrespect, by word or deed, the woman in your life, you need to change your running crowd.
- If you always mean to help your partners become better men but instead you keep ending up worse, you need to change your running crowd.
- If you're committed to keeping your buddies and hiding the woman you love from them, you need to change your running crowd.

Changing your running crowd is not for the sake of gaining her love, but it's because you take seriously setting up the right conditions for your relationship to flourish. If your running crowd doesn't help that or actually gets in the way of it, you can't afford that crowd.

THE BOTTOM LINE

Men at work: Be honest with yourself about your friends. Stop being available to run with the wrong crowd. Tell the brothers you have absolutely no business spending time with why you must pull back, even though it's hard to do.

The benefits: Taking the bold step of rethinking who your friends are for the sake of yourself and the health of your relationship is the kind of willingness to sacrifice that demonstrates sincere commitment. Sacrifice and commitment are the means by which you develop true intimacy.

The costs: To remove yourself from the people and activities that get in the way of your growth as an individual and as a relationship partner may feel like you are selling out your buddies, depriving yourself of some fun, or being manipulated by your woman's taste in friends for you.

59. ▲ ■ ● ◆ ◗ *Apologize with Words*

To the man who loves me:
When you've let me down, your apologies mean a lot to me.
It takes a real man to say "I'm sorry." Though there are a
million ways you could show me how sorry you are, I really
do want to hear you say those two little words to me.

—From the Black woman you love

Let's be real about it. At some point—probably at several points—you will blow it. You'll try to do something in the name of love and for the sake of the Black woman in your life and you'll fail—perhaps miserably. She'll feel let down or angry, or weary, or a combination of all three, and you'll feel guilty, embarrassed, and exposed. Rotten feelings all around.

There are countless ways that human imperfection shows itself in a loving relationship. You, and every man or woman on the planet, can be counted on to disappoint, offend, or disgust each other at some time. But we also need to be able to count on each other to acknowledge our mess-ups and apologize for them too. Like it or not, it's a job that is most effectively done with words—and plainly spoken, nondefensive words, at that!

Women tend to be verbal. They place a high value on words, spoken and heard. Men, on the other hand, are often very content to rely heavily on nonverbal expression. With apologies, leaving it at the nonverbal level seldom works in her best interest or yours. Use words.

When, instead of *saying* "I'm sorry" (and why you are), you resort to apology alternatives, like doing something especially nice for her as a kind of penance, buying her something as a payoff, or just privately committing to yourself to do better next time—you leave out the essential ingredient that matters most to the Black woman you love: humility. Because humility is exactly what it takes to open your mouth and admit you were wrong. Pride and arrogance are opposite of humility. They require men to take an oath of silence after a mess-up. As if the failure somehow didn't really happen if you don't mention it.

One of the things men most hate to hear women say is that their men are full of pride, arrogance, and insensitivity. When they've said it, believe me, a big part of the hurt that motivated it was around their man's failure to adequately apologize. To her that can feel like a worse offense than the original one, because it adds insult to injury.

THE BOTTOM LINE

Men at work: A "good man" puts down his fear of being seen as a failure and chooses to love his woman by saying "I'm sorry" when he really is and when he is committed to a different course of action the next time. Work on both speaking the words and changing the offending behaviors. Never settle for just one or the other.

The benefits: Verbal apologies are actually the quickest and cleanest way to communicate what you are sorry for and how much your woman's feelings mean to you. The possibility of your mess-up lingering around in the shadows, providing her ammunition for future attacks against you, is dramatically lessened. If you'll get it out, you'll get it over with much quicker. It's not attaining perfection, but how you handle your imperfections that shows you to be a man of courage and integrity.

The costs: You'll feel like there's a little meter inside you adding up each and every "I'm sorry." It'll make you not want to say it before you feel you have too many.

60. ▲ ■ ◗ *Resist the Sugar Daddy in You*

To the man who loves me:
Now, don't get me wrong. I do enjoy all those wonderful romantic things you do for me and everything you've given me. You're very generous, and I'm very impressed. But maybe you've been generous for the wrong reasons. Maybe you think it takes all that to keep me. Wrong!

—From the Black woman you love

Having stuff and being able to give it to your woman can be tremendously appealing to men. There is such a satisfying jolt of power and significance to be gained from dispensing material goodies to the Black woman you love. It is the ego stroke of being Santa Claus, her wealthy benefactor Daddy, and "The Bank" all rolled into one. And when that's what it's all about, then it's not about her very much at all. It's about you and your conscious or unconscious search for significance by casting yourself in the role of her Sugar Daddy.

Some women may love it and they'll give you loads of admiration, approval, and applause in exchange for the various baubles, bangles, and beads you dole out to them. But eventually you'll get tired of "love" that costs so much and returns so little. In fact, many Black women couldn't care less about your trinkets. These days they've managed to get those for themselves. Instead, they want you, your devotion, your companionship, commitment, and affection far more than they need your stuff.

Quiet as it's kept, Sugar Daddies would much rather be loved for who they are, not just for what they hand out. If you're one, and you suddenly terminate your Sweet Daddy Macking and change the dynamics of the relationship, you may discover, however, that with some women it *was* the gifts she was after and not the giver. But if you keep on being Big Daddy Greenback you'll lose respect for yourself and begin to despise her, when you see that her love for you only reaches as far as what you've got in your hands or your pockets.

Resist the Sugar Daddy urge anyway. To give generously to your woman with the goal of blessing and benefiting the person you love is one thing. But to do that exact same giving with the number-one goal being to get more of her awe and admiration, thus boosting your sense of significance, is not only expensive, but it's selfish, and more than a little foolish. Selfishness and foolishness have no place in your love life.

If you've got a bit of the Sugar Daddy in you:

- Learn how to show up without having to bring something in your hands for her every time.
- Don't take all her financial complaints as hints that you must do something about them.
- Don't make promises that are based on what you only hope you can provide her but currently have no way to do.

• Don't lie to yourself about who your Sugar Daddying is really for. First, last, and always, it's for you.

THE BOTTOM LINE

Men at work: Go ahead and have that dreaded conversation with yourself, and with your woman, where you acknowledge, and assume all responsibilities for, your Sugar Daddy ways. Lovingly, yet firmly, announce that you are through shopping for significance by paying for love.

The benefits: You and the Black woman in your life will be able to clear away the superficial material "tokens" of love and get down to the real thing, love that is based on the emotional and spiritual bond between a man and a woman— rather than the one-way flow of cash and commodities.

The costs: If you stop playing Sugar Daddy you run the risk of finding out how little you mean to her and how much your stuff does.

61. ▲ ■ ● ◆ ◗ Never Play with the Word "Marriage"

To the man who loves me:
Marriage, marriage, marriage. I've heard you use the word over and over now. Over and over I still wonder what exactly you have in mind when you say it.

—From the Black woman you love

As you work to get better and better at putting your private thoughts and deepest feelings into words for the Black woman you love, I urge you to pause and truly hear this word of caution: Don't even think about uttering the word "marriage" to her until you're dead serious about it. Even if you think you might perhaps, one day, some way, we'll see, be headed that way, wait until you know you know or otherwise you'll be playing with the idea and she'll begin to think you're playing with her.

- Don't drop hints or raise her hopes.
- Don't play-act the possibility. Say it and mean it, then either do it, or don't.
- Don't use the word to manipulate, reward, or pacify her.
- Don't try to talk yourself into it by talking about it with her.

Marriage is the ultimate, intimate, exclusive, and long-term commitment between a man and a woman. For a woman, intimacy, exclusivity, and permanence are the three essential elements that confirm the strength and security of your love for her. When you start talking marriage and you're nowhere near marriage-ready, you've started constructing a high-rise building in her mind without bothering to lay the foundation. When it comes tumbling down, she'll be buried in the rubble.

Of course it's important to have some dialogue on the subject of marriage before you're down on your knees with a ring in your hand and a proposal on your lips, but at the just-talking-about-it stage, it's best to keep your words few and resist the temptation to spout anything that she could take as a promise. Because men are so goal-oriented and task-driven it seems that if you really are feeling strongly about her and the relationship, you really should get busy identifying a goal, looking at the possibility, and watching to see what develops.

And when men are in that mode they get a lot of satisfaction from talking about their ideas in order to analyze, troubleshoot, and evaluate them. It's fine to do that, but it's foolish to do it with her. Watch it: You may hear your words as an idea that you are considering. She may hear those same words as an idea you have confirmed.

THE BOTTOM LINE

Men at work: Do some serious initial observation and assessment of you and your mate's marriageability and marriage-readiness before you begin to talk matrimony with her. Until it's more than a maybe with you, explore the possibilities and think aloud about marrying her only in the company of your own support network, and separate from your woman. If you do broach the subject even in the most preliminary and commitment-free way, take pains to clearly communicate where you are and where you aren't about marriage (only daydreaming for now, or curious but cautious, or serious and inquiring, and so forth).

The benefits: Clarity. Avoiding premature or indefinite marriage talk will circumvent one of the most potentially destructive kinds of misunderstandings. This way you can't be found guilty of "relational fraud" and violation of an implied verbal agreement. You'll both be reading off the same page about marriage. She won't have to endure the pain and embarrassment of feeling set up by your careless words that offer her a vision of matrimony that may never materialize.

The costs: If you resist toying with the idea of marriage, you will sacrifice all the fun of playing pretend games with your woman. It really does work for you to try an idea on for size first, and speculating about it out loud helps you do just that. But it can cost your woman far too much in unfulfilled hopes and emotional upheaval.

62. ■ ● *Stop Comparing Paychecks*

To the man who loves me:
I sometimes wonder who first came up with the idea that
how much money we make gets to determine who we should
love and who we shouldn't. I hope we both continue trying
in our own ways to be successful people. But even if the level
of success we each achieve differs, that shouldn't have any-
thing to do with us staying together. Please don't let it.

—From the Black woman you love

One of the walls that separates Black women and the men who love them has come about because somewhere along the way many of them started practicing a very destructive habit: comparing paychecks. As if little numbers on big checks is the way to decide who deserves respect and who has the most rights and privileges in a relationship.

Lately, this obsession with measuring how much is in one's heart and soul by how much is in his or her pocket or purse has made some Black women afraid to admit and celebrate their material successes. It's also made some of the men who love them become humiliated and embarrassed when their numbers don't match or exceed their mate's. The fact is, the true value of a man or woman, and the relationship between them, is measured by the character and qualities of the two individuals, not the job they do and how much they earn for doing it. When you get hung up on those superficial matters, you'll fail to look deeper at a potential or present mate and you'll fail to discover the amount of character and commitment they possess within. And if you don't know their riches or poverty within, you'll stay distracted by the blue-collar/white-collar, "first and fifteenth," dollars-and-cents differences that may tempt you to disqualify yourself from such a woman. Or as bad is pursuing and remaining with a character- and commitment-poor Black woman *because* she's a high earner. Either way it's an insult to one or both of you.

Careful, every prosperous Black woman isn't damning you because you are not equally prosperous. Nor is every Black woman who has little materially requiring that you "bring the bank." Certainly there are some like that, but that is not the norm. You'll have to stick around and look around awhile to know which kind you're dealing with before you draw that conclusion about her and move forward or pull back from her.

THE BOTTOM LINE

Men at work: Work as hard as you can to excel at what you do and the compensation you get for it. Don't compare your earnings to hers. Define success as doing the best work you possibly can and getting the most you can for doing it. Compare your paycheck to your own effort, potential, and opportunity, and nothing else.

The benefits: Resisting paycheck obsession prior to marriage gives you a wider range of potential mates because you're not using pay stubs, credit reports, and investment portfolios to qualify or disqualify a potential partner. In a marital relationship, you can enjoy the closeness and interdependence that comes from living as if all the dollars you make are not his or her dollars but "*our* dollars."

The costs: Because men tend to define themselves largely by what they do, and the rewards they get for it, keeping paycheck measures of financial success secondary may be difficult for you. It may not be easy to switch to some other measure of your success.

63. ▲ ■ ● ◆) *Take Good Care of Your Kids*

To the man who loves me:
I enjoy so much watching you with the kids. You know them so well and just how to talk to them to make them feel loved and cared for. You can look in their eyes and tell that they know they can always count on you. You may never know how much that means to me.

—From the Black woman you love

If you've brought children into this imperfect and sometimes threatening world, you have signed on to be the most important man in the world of another living soul. It's neither part-time nor temporary. It's not just about what you do, it's about who you are before them. It's a long-term commitment to protect and to provide the resources—material, physical, spiritual, and emotional—that they will constantly need in order to flourish.

No matter how they got here or where they live, your children deserve your attentive, consistent, self-sacrificing presence in their lives on a daily basis. When you give them that, and not just your tender emotions and well-intentioned promises, your love for them becomes and remains alive, active, and visible—to them and to the Black woman you love.

The way you take care of your children reveals to your woman like nothing else can the depth of your capacity for love and commitment. Should you have little concern for your own flesh and blood she may reasonably conclude that you couldn't possibly have that much for her either.

These days the vast number of Black women raising children alone or with the father's "maybe today, maybe tomorrow" involvement has left many women exhausted, deeply disappointed, and full of mistrust.

You provide a healing touch to your woman and to Black women everywhere when you allow absolutely nothing to stop you from working toward perfection in caring for your children. Without excuses, in spite of distractions, and free of selfishness and blaming.

THE BOTTOM LINE

Men at work: If it's not possible to live in the same household with your children, at least live in the same town with them, even if it requires radically altering your life. That way you are available for daily, face-to-face interaction with them. Reestablish, recommit, or consistently maintain the highest possible levels of physical, spiritual, emotional, social, and financial involvement in their lives. Let what you promise to your children and to your woman (about your children) be what you actually deliver, and keep delivering, no matter what.

The benefits: Aside from the obvious benefits to your children, you will offer the woman you love the most compelling evidence that you are a man whose love can be trusted to include sacrifice and long-term commitment.

The costs: Having to work so hard to demonstrate your love for your kids' sake as well as your mate's sometimes will feel like too many people needing too much from you. Also, expect it to be harder to maintain a high level of commitment and involvement with your children when your woman and your kids' mother are not the same person. It can mean dealing with envy, strain, and a tug-of-war over your time and attentions.

64. ■ ● ◆ *Remember the Big Events*

To the man who loves me:
Thank you so much. I know I get excited as the kids do about
all our special occasions. And I know they don't necessarily
mean as much to you. But I get so much joy out of the way
you let me go completely berserk celebrating and you join
right in.

—From the Black woman you love

Most of the dates she has circled on her calendar may mean far more to her than to you, but if you're the man who loves her, you'd do well to remember them and enthusiastically celebrate them as well. The big events of course are her birthday, your anniversaries, holidays, the first day of this thing or the last day of that thing, and other milestones in her life or in the history of your relationship. To the Black woman you love these special occasions and the rituals and traditions that go with them are the perfect opportunities to celebrate what matters most to her: the joy and the significance of your shared life together.

When you remember the big events and honor them with your enthusiastic participation, you confirm to her that in this fast-moving life there are moments that belong to the two of you alone, and they hold status far above all other days. The big events are symbols of some of the specialness of your lives on this crowded planet. When you remember by yourself, and don't have to be reminded every time, you are in position to take some initiative in the way the occasions will be honored. That's much better than merely following along as a silent partner who appears as if he couldn't care less what, if anything, happens on these occasions.

Like it or not, a part of her identity is wrapped up in the big events of her life. When you remember and celebrate them you recognize and reaffirm those parts of her that the big events represent. Her birthday: the one day when you reaffirm that she is the leading lady, the queen, the hero of your life. It's about her, and when you recognize and celebrate it she knows it's fine with you that it's about her. Valentine's Day and your anniversary: when you recognize and reaffirm your love for each other as well as celebrate from whence you've come together and where you're headed.

Don't let the rituals, traditions, and ceremonies that go along with you and your woman's way of celebrating slip away. As the years fly past keep creatively and enthusiastically involved in observing the big events. It's not how much money you spend, it's all about the zeal you bring to the celebration.

THE BOTTOM LINE

Men at work: Mark your calendar well in advance and you be the one who first brings the big events up and makes plans for them to be bigger and bigger.

The benefits: Celebrations that you don't get swallowed up in because of your guilt or have forgotten or not planned anything; instead you have some creative input and thus some control. You win and so does she.

The costs: Big events seem never to end. When one goes away another is just around the corner.

65. ■ • *Become Her Best Mirror*

To the man who loves me:
I don't care much about what "everybody else" has to say about me and how I look. Knowing that you, my man, find me beautiful and what you find beautiful about me are what really matter to me.

—From the Black woman you love

Even if she's the most secure, self-assured, and popular Black woman, knowing that the man who loves her is impressed with what he sees when he looks at her means the world to her. But what she prizes even more is when you tell her about the beauty that you see. If you're willing to become her best mirror, you'll be more than any looking glass where she'll most delight in seeing her image reflected. It will be found there in your approving eyes and admiring words.

The Black woman you love, or one day will, relishes every kind of reminder and reassurance that she is desirable to you. It's not need, insecurity, or sheer vanity that makes her yearn for your approval and appreciation of her outer beauty. It comes from that part of a woman's nature that delights in knowing there is one person on this planet to whom she can boldly bring all the various parts of herself and that they can be found wonderfully acceptable, desirable, and pursueable.

You're her favorite mirror when you consistently:

- Rush to point out her most attractive features rather than criticize her flaws.
- Notice and commend her efforts to enhance her beauty.
- Brag to others, especially in her presence, about how gorgeous she is.
- Find her completely embraceable before she's made up her face and "whipped" her hair.
- Don't make her have to assume, guess, or imagine that she's attractive to you, but tell her instead.
- Don't compare her looks or attributes to those of any other woman.
- Encourage her about a part of her appearance about which she's very sensitive.
- Thank her for making you look so good.

She shouldn't have to look like Whitney or Naomi or Tyra to merit your highest praise, any more than you must look like Denzel, Wesley, or Billy D to get hers. You needn't lie to her. That will get old fast. Rather, find the many or few marks of her beauty and tell her over and over what you see.

THE BOTTOM LINE

Men at work: Find out at least one major and two minor things about her appearance to compliment each day. Keep one or two ready for when she asks you for them. Should you be given the opportunity to make a suggestion or voice a constructive criticism about her appearance, sandwich it between two glowing compliments.

The benefits: A woman who is confident that she is attractive and desirable to her man carries a unique and powerful self-confidence and openness. She'll perform at higher levels within and outside her relationship with you. Your praise helps her to become the kind of self-assured, high-performance woman most attractive to you.

The costs: It will be hard for her to fully appreciate your compliments about her outer beauty very long if you seldom (or never) mention what you find attractive about her inner beauty. Also, you will find it difficult to reflect her beauty to her when she makes appearance choices that you hate (like hairstyle, clothes, weight). The fact is, the more you lavishly and sincerely praise what you do like, the more attention she'll pay to the things you'd like her to change or improve.

66. ▲ ■ ● ◆ ◗ Don't Let Pride Rob You of the Help You Need

To the man who loves me:
It's not criticism, it's concern. Believe it or not I love you and I can't sit comfortably by and watch you go under when you don't have to. You and our life together mean too much to me for me to be able to stand that.

—From the Black woman you love

One of the things that has made Black women sometimes reluctant to put their full confidence in the men who love them is the men's often stubborn refusal to seek help when it's clear they desperately need it. Women instinctively tend to call out for specialized help when they are in a specialized jam. They are bewildered and frankly scared to death by the man who's willing to go under and take her with him before he'll acknowledge a need and ask guidance or assistance from someone who has something or knows something that he doesn't. If you've ever known such a man or seen him in the mirror, you know he's got PRIDE written all over him.

Pride is image-obsession fueled by false and ultimately self-destructive notions of what it means to be a man. The pride that keeps men from seeking help is based on the lie that a man ought to be able to handle every facet of his life (and especially his love life) by using his own resources. If he can't, pride erroneously argues that he's a failure and not a real man. Men instinctively avoid people, places, or things which might make them feel like a failure. Unless you recognize pride's lies and deceptions for what they are and accept the truth that sometimes needing someone else's help is a given, you'll be robbed of the opportunity to get exactly what you need, when you need it.

It's hard enough for some men to ask a friend for something as simple as help in solving a transportation problem or some assistance in polishing up a résumé or figuring out the best job option. Your woman grieves for you and for herself as she witnesses you opting to do without, rather than reach out, in these plain, everyday matters. But her grief is multiplied a thousand times when in the crisis you won't seek needed professional help like that of a financial advisor, a doctor, a therapist or a marriage counselor, a minister or an attorney. Instead, you're willing to suffer and allow her to suffer with you the slow death or rapid decline of your finances, your health, your emotional well-being, your relationship, or your family. And all this to save face and avoid any damage to your ego's lust for significance through supreme self-sufficiency.

The pride robs you of far more than it benefits you. It costs you in terms of her resentment, anxiety, and misery. It costs you directly because when you fail to seek help, you're likely to keep suffering multiple, irretrievable losses and ultimately the loss of your own self-respect.

THE BOTTOM LINE

Men at work: Don't deny, pretend, or tolerate the paralysis of analysis. When you need help (or even think you do), say no to your pride and get the help you need from the best possible places you have access to. Demonstrate to your mate that you love her too much to allow your undealt-with needs to become a crisis for her.

The benefits: Freedom from the bondage of prideful image-protecting. The benefits you'll derive from other people's expertise and abilities. Your woman will feel more secure, knowing that you are the kind of man who gets what he needs to take care of himself and those he loves.

The costs: That uncomfortably humbling feeling that comes with admitting you have a need and pursuing someone else's help to meet it.

67. ▲ ■ ● ◆ ❍
Love Her in Ways You Want Your Son to Imitate

To the man who loves me:
No matter how hard it gets, just don't give up trying to make
our relationship solid. We can't afford to screw up at this.
Like it or not, our children are becoming who we are.

—From the Black woman you love

It doesn't matter whether any of them are your actual flesh and blood, or whether they live at your address, or call you Daddy. Our sons are watching you. They are paying close attention even when you're not paying attention to what you say, how you say it, and what you actually do in the name of love for the Black woman in your life. For some "man-in-the-making," or several, you are their teacher, textbook, and role model on the subject of how to love a Black woman. Like it or not, these boys will learn more from how you live the lesson than from whatever you might say about it.

Treating Black women with dignity, tenderness, truthfulness is what it takes. It requires the application of wisdom, creativity, and skillfulness before our sons can be turned loose on the next generation of our daughters. Aside from the essential rightness of loving your woman with care, aside from how it edifies her and benefits her, is the grave obligation you have to equip your son, and all our sons, to do it as well. Will he get it if he patterns himself after you?

Too often your brothers of this generation did not have the benefit of constant, up-close role models around to demonstrate the finer points of:

- Listening to a woman when what she's saying is true, but embarrassing or ego-deflating.
- Speaking about her, even in her absence, in ways that honor and esteem her.
- Protecting her from mistreatment.
- Honestly telling her your limitations, but always giving her your best.
- Not being intimidated by her strength.
- Letting her have welcome access to your innermost thoughts, feelings, and aspirations.
- Adding to rather than taking from her sense of security when you can, and always being sensitive to what makes her sad or afraid.
- Valuing and accepting her as exactly who you want in your life, even if she's not exactly what you wanted.
- Keeping your complaints few and your expressions of affection frequent.
- Measuring love by what you give, not just what you get.

THE BOTTOM LINE

Men at work: Constantly ask yourself and demand an answer to this question: "Am I treating this woman in a way that I'd be proud for my son to imitate?" Make changes accordingly.

The benefits: The joy and satisfaction of working hard to become the best kind of man to the Black woman you love and literally shaping the life of the next generation by raising a high standard of masculine love.

The costs: The awesome burden of influencing somebody else's life other than your own, and, having accepted that, the tendency to ache with guilt over your past failures.

68. *Don't Let Your Love Life Become Your Whole Life*

To the man who loves me:
I used to be flattered by the feeling that I was the center of
your universe and that you didn't seem to need anyone or
anything else in your life. Now, to be honest, your needing
me so much feels like a heavy weight on my shoulders. Some-
thing's not right with this.

—From the Black woman you love

For a healthy man in a healthy relationship, there are two parts of you that together make the whole. One is your desire for the sense of connectedness that sharing your life with your woman brings. The other is your need to stand separate and apart from her in the independent side of your nature. Your desire for intimacy is not a curse. Your craving for independence is not a crime. But if either of the two is out of balance all kinds of problems can and will result. If most everything you value, pursue, or accomplish in your life is connected to, or initiated by, her, you have surrendered your identity as an individual. And if you are not able to be happy, whole, and content apart from your relationship with her, she will eventually find you to be more of a burden than a blessing. Because when your love life becomes practically your whole life, you don't have enough life of your own to share with anyone else.

It's not intimacy, it's dependence that has a man seeking virtually all his identity, self-esteem, and companionship needs from one source, his woman.

You'll know if you're dependent on her if her approval, her expectations, and her constant presence are your preoccupations, if they are nearly all you think about, talk about, and do anything about. If these are all connected to pleasing or keeping her, your world revolves too much around her, and the smothering effect of it will turn her off, and eventually run her off.

Black women admire and are highly attracted to signs of strength, reasonable self-sufficiency, and self-confidence in you. Though they want to be included in your life and hold a highly cherished place in it, they don't want the burden of having to give you a life. When you march to her drumbeat and not your own, that indicates to her that you are a needy man with insufficient internal resources. You will at best elicit her motherly devotion and sympathy but never her romantic love, admiration, and respect. To show her otherwise and, more importantly, to open the narrow confines of your life:

- Make and keep some friendships of your own, not just ones you inherited from her.
- Discover and pursue the things that will enhance your personal, professional, and spiritual life without waiting for her direction or motivation.
- Resist the pursuit of her total agreement and endorsement of your every idea, opinion, and plan in order for you to act upon them.
- Strengthen your ability to tolerate being alone. Your social and recreational life should not be limited to her company or her arrangements.

THE BOTTOM LINE

Men at work: Maintain a healthy independence along with the shared life of intimacy with your woman. Never abandon one for the other or you'll end up losing both.

The benefits: If you refuse to allow your woman and your relationship to become or remain the sole focus of your life, and you maintain some of your independent interests and pursuits, you are far more attractive to her than the man whose whole life revolves around her. For your sake, you'll stop using love and your lover as a drug, lulling you to sluggish inactivity. You will regain the balance between your purposeful independence and healthy intimacy by choice, not by necessity.

The costs: Your woman could be resistant to your changing your style on her abruptly, even if she has secretly loathed your dependent ways. It may have turned out to be a sign to her of your all-consuming devotion. She may feel threatened by any manifestation of your independence. And when she feels threatened, you may have to fight the urge to give up your life again and put her back at the center of your existence.

69. ▲ *Stay*

To the man who loves me:
When it's all said and done, a love that's here today and
gone tomorrow is just not worth it to me. I know that if we
really plan to be with each other there will always be good
times and not so good times. I can deal with that, but only
if I know you plan to be here, in this with me, through
whatever comes our way.

—From the Black woman you love

Even if you could perfectly perform all the advice in this book making available to the Black woman you love the best your mind, body, and spirit have to offer, in the final analysis it wouldn't matter very much if you are not a man who sticks around. Sometimes the hardest expression of your love for your woman will be rising to the challenge to stay when you feel that powerful urge to drift or flee. Choosing to stay anyway is your love at its most disciplined and determined. Staying involves keeping your focus, and maintaining your efforts on behalf of the relationship instead of letting yourself become distracted or "gone" without actually leaving.

There are an endless number of reasons why your staying power may wane at certain points as you work to build and maintain a relationship. Though all of them aren't justifiable reasons to pull up stakes and move on, they are real and persuasive, and you would do well to pay attention to them. Otherwise they are sure to try to control you rather than you controlling them. Don't be surprised if you get "itchy feet" when:

- You're bored. It may seem you know all her little crooks and crevices and there's little possibility of thrilling discovery and exciting conquest left to be had together. You're simply tired of her and want new frontiers.
- You're disappointed. It turns out she actually does not fulfill your perfect fantasy of what your woman and your relationship were supposed to look like.
- You're tired. When your relationship begins to feel like way too much work and like the burden of it is all on your shoulders, you will yearn for a vacation, perhaps a permanent one.
- You're distracted. The grass looks greener elsewhere. Some other woman or goal or way of life grabs your attention and beckons you to come and bring your all. You feel confined: The daily demands and discipline of your relationship with her sometimes make it seem like you're serving a life sentence in a cramped cell.

Your feelings are real and they may even be based on some actual flaws in your woman or your relationship, but feelings alone shouldn't be allowed to dictate your decision to stay or to go. If they do you'll become (or continue to be) somebody who spends his life packing and unpacking—promising your love, then taking it back.

When many Black women have been willing to be painfully honest, they have admitted that some of their worst fears about loving us is the possibility that your staying power will dissipate.

They end up crushed by the idea that they weren't enough to make you want to remain in spite of the inevitable challenges and restless feelings that tempt you to go. That kind of rejection, perhaps having been rerun countless times before, has led many Black women to put up a protective veneer, become suspicious of you and openly derisive of all men, and of Black men in particular. Your departures—even your logically and sensitively explained ones—wound them deeply. Not unlike the way their criticism and disrespect wounds you.

All courtships are not destined to be permanent relationships. And, no, you don't have to give your life away to a girlfriend who's all wrong for you and you for her. But stick around long enough to know exactly why you're choosing to leave and to make sure it is a mature decision driven by truth and wisdom and not just your impulsivity and self-centeredness.

To those men who have already vowed till death do us part, I'll make it simple: Put your feelings in their place and recommit to stay and do all you possibly can to make the marriage the best it possibly can be. There should be nearly nothing that changes that.

THE BOTTOM LINE

Men at work: Examine your own history and your patterns of entering and exiting relationships with women. Consider how much self-centeredness and a "never-satisfied" attitude have played a part in your departures. Honestly, diligently work to do the opposite in your current or next relationship.

The benefits: Aside from the obvious benefit to your woman's sense of security, making a serious commitment to stay will model to other men and our sons a love with that all too rare staying power.

The costs: Feeling the restless feelings and not automatically "medicating" them by leaving the premises.

70. ▲ ■ ● ◆ ▶ *Keep on Loving Her Even if You Don't Always "Get It"*

To the man who loves me:
I suspect we'll never have each other completely figured out.
I don't think I even want us to. If the way I am sometimes is
hard for you to understand, let's not worry about that. We
may wonder about each other sometimes, but then we'll
never bore each other.

—From the Black woman you love

Even if you carefully memorize every piece of advice contained in this book and follow it to the letter, you will find Black women (and especially your own) will still, from time to time, stare at you with a furrowed brow and an exasperated tone and declare: "You just don't get it, do you."

And because it will still sometimes be hard to figure out what she is talking about and what in the world she wants, you could be inclined to agree with her and answer back: "You're right, I *don't* get it!"

In some sense the ways of women and what it takes to love them will always be a mystery to you. They will eternally possess some confusing "X factors" that you just won't understand. Don't sweat it. You can love them just fine even when you don't always "get it."

Men can't stand not being able to thoroughly explain the things that baffle them. That's why little boys eventually break open their favorite toy to explore its insides and find answers to the mysteries of how the thing works. To men every question ought to have an answer. And if a man has a question, he feels he'd better get the answer, or he'll melt, evaporate, or pass out and die of "terminal bewilderment." The truth is there are some things about women for which no neat, tidy answers exist. They are, and to some extent will always remain, a mystery to men.

One of the greatest attractions between men and women is the fact that they can never fully sum each other up. No matter what profound discoveries you make, on some questions you will still be left groping in the dark for answers. Getting bored with each other is much less likely to happen when a little mystery remains between you. Learn to tolerate it.

Don't get nervous. Don't bang your head against the wall. Don't give up on Black women or on yourself. When you can't understand her *and* love her, then just love her.

Relax. Some answers to her mysterious ways will come later and some not at all. If you accept that, not being able to "get it" about something she did, said, or meant and why and what she really wants from you won't be so frustrating. Keep right on loving her anyway. She'll prove to be just understandable enough to grab your attention and just mysterious enough to keep it.

THE BOTTOM LINE

Men at work: Work on loving your woman in spite of her unexplainable ways and the mysterious differences between her style and yours. Whenever you become baffled, impatient, or at a loss to make sense of her, say to yourself, "I don't get it. And, at this moment, that'll have to be okay."

The benefits: Relief from the burdensome pressure to fully comprehend every minute detail of your woman's personality, behavior, motivation, and style of relating to you. You give her the liberating permission to remain somewhat a mystery to you and you give yourself permission not to have to turn romance into research.

The costs: Feeling slightly stupid that she accuses you of not understanding her, and having to agree that, at that moment, you really don't.

For Booking Information

How to Love a Black Woman and *How to Love a Black Man* were inspired by the many men and women throughout the country who have experienced powerful transformations in their lives after attending one of Ronn Elmore's highly popular seminars.

Dr. Elmore is much sought after for conferences, seminars, communications skills workshops, and other speaking engagements inspiring his audiences on a wide range of topics related to love, marriage, the family, and personal success.

To schedule an event:

The Ronn Elmore Group
The Trinity Building
333 W. Florence Ave. Suite 212
Inglewood, CA 90301

Attention: Booking Manager
(213) 732-0250